MW01097113

CONTENTS

CHAPTER 1 - ALGEBRA

1.1. – ORDER OF OPERATIONS

1. $5 + 3 \cdot 2 =$

2. $2 \cdot 3 - (-3) =$

3. $-5 \cdot 5 - (-8) \cdot 2 =$

4. $-2 - 5 - (-2) + 2 =$

5. $(-2)(-5) - (-2) \cdot 2 =$

6. $25 \cdot 2 - 7 =$

7. $15 + 4 / 2 =$

8. $14 / 7 + 3 \cdot 6 =$

9. $5 / 5 - 30 / 2 \cdot 5 =$

10. $1 + 4 / 2 - 8 / 4 \cdot 5 =$

11. $20 / 4 / 2 + 4 =$

12. $12 \cdot (2 + 3) =$

13. $5(3 \cdot 2 / 3 \cdot 2) + 2 =$

14. $1 / 2 + 3 / 2 =$

15. $6 / 3 - 20 / 10 =$

16. $5(1 + 3 \cdot 2) + 2 / 2 - 8 / 4 =$

17. $(15 + 3) \cdot 2 - 2 =$

18. $0 / 5 + 3 \cdot 2 =$

19. $5 / 0 + 3 \cdot 2 =$

20. $(1 + 1) \cdot (2 - 2) \cdot (4 \cdot 5 \cdot 5) =$

21. $(5 + 3) \cdot 2 =$

22. $(5 \cdot 3) \cdot 2 =$

23. $5 \cdot (3 \cdot 2) =$

24. $5 \cdot 3 \cdot 2 =$

25. $100 / 2^2 + 21 / 3 =$

26. $(2 + 1)^2 / 3 + 13 =$

27. $2(3^2 - 4 / 2)^2 - 1 \cdot 3 =$

28. $3(1 - 4 / 2^2)^2 - 4^2 / 3 =$

29. $10(2^4 / 2 - 1^2 + 1) / 2 =$

30. $2 + 3(2 - 20 / 2^2)^2 - (5^2 + 3) / 2 =$

31. $5 / 0 =$

32. $0 / 4 =$

33. $0 / 0 =$

34. $(2 + 4) \cdot 5^2 - 2 / 2 =$

35. $-1 \cdot 5^2 - 2^2 + (-2)^{3 - 1 \cdot 2} =$

36. $\left(-2^2 - 2\right)^2 \cdot (-2)^{1-1} =$

37. $(4 - 5 \cdot 2) / 2 - 1 =$

1.2. – INTRODUCTION TO FRACTIONS

1. Given the following circle, divide it to 2 equal pieces and shade $\frac{1}{2}$

2. Given the following circle divide it to 3 equal pieces and shade $\frac{1}{3}$

3. Given the following circle, divide it to 4 equal pieces and shade $\frac{1}{4}$

4. Given the following circle, divide it to 5 equal pieces and shade $\frac{1}{5}$

5. Given the following circle, divide it to 6 equal pieces and shade $\frac{1}{6}$

6. Given the following circle, divide it to 7 equal pieces and shade $\frac{1}{7}$

7. Given the following circle, divide it to 8 equal pieces and shade $\frac{1}{8}$

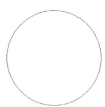

8. Given the following circle, divide it to 9 equal pieces and shade $\frac{1}{9}$

9. Given the following circle, divide it to 10 equal pieces and shade $\frac{1}{10}$

10. Given the following circle, divide it to 3 equal pieces and shade $\dfrac{2}{3}$

11. Given the following circle, divide it to 4 equal pieces and shade $\dfrac{2}{4}$

12. Given the following circle, divide it to 4 equal pieces and shade $\dfrac{3}{4}$

13. Given the following circle, divide it to 5 equal pieces and shade $\dfrac{2}{5}$

14. Given the following circle, divide it to 6 equal pieces and shade $\dfrac{5}{6}$

15. Given the following circle, divide it to 8 equal pieces and shade $\dfrac{5}{8}$

16. Given the following circle, divide it to 5 equal pieces and shade $\dfrac{4}{5}$

17. Given the following circle, divide it to 9 equal pieces and shade $\dfrac{4}{9}$

18. What fraction of the following circle is shaded:

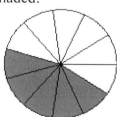

19. What fraction of the following circle is shaded:

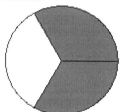

20. What fraction of the following circle is shaded:

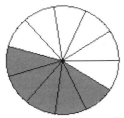

21. What fraction of the following circle is shaded:

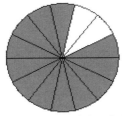

22. What fraction of the following circle is shaded:

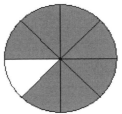

23. What fraction of the following circle is shaded:

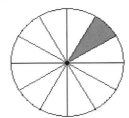

24. What fraction of the following table is shaded:

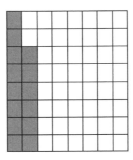

25. What fraction of the following table is shaded:

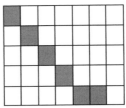

26. What fraction of the following table is shaded?

27. What fraction is shaded?

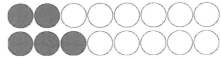

28. What fraction is shaded?

29. What fraction is shaded?

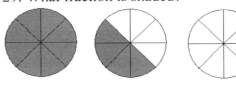

30. What fraction is shaded?

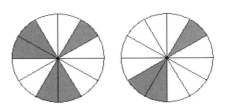

31. There were 12 cookies in the jar. John ate 5, write down the fraction of cookies john ate and the fraction that is left in the jar.

32. Lia ate 3 cookies that represented $\frac{3}{4}$ of the cookies in the jar. Write down the number of cookies in the jar before she ate. Make a sketch to show answer.

33. Rami ate $\frac{2}{5}$ of the cookies in the jar, Melissa ate $\frac{1}{4}$ of the cookies. Who ate more? Invent an imaginary jar with a number of cookies that will make the problem easy to solve.

34. How much is $\frac{1}{2}$ of 2? Shade to show your answer:

35. How much is $\frac{1}{3}$ of 2? Shade to show your answer:

36. How much is $\frac{1}{4}$ of 2? Shade to show your answer:

37. How much is $\frac{1}{5}$ of 2? Shade to show your answer:

38. How much is $\frac{1}{3}$ of 5? Shade in 2 different ways to show your answer:

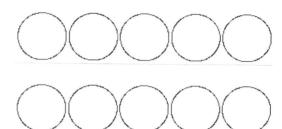

39. How much is $\frac{2}{5}$ of 4? Shade in 2 different ways to show your answer:

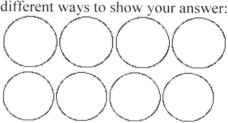

40. Sketch $\frac{3}{2}$ circles:

41. Sketch $\frac{5}{3}$ circles:

42. Sketch $\frac{7}{4}$ circles:

43. Sketch $\frac{8}{4}$ circles:

44. Sketch $\frac{7}{5}$ circles:

45. Sketch $\frac{8}{3}$ circles:

46. Nathan ate $\frac{2}{7}$ of the cookies in the jar, Melissa ate $\frac{1}{3}$ of the cookies. Who ate more? Invent an imaginary jar with a number of cookies that will make the problem easy to solve.

47. Write down the missing number(s) between 0 and 1:

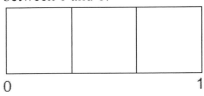

48. Write down the missing number(s) between 0 and 1:

49. Write down the missing number(s) between 0 and 1:

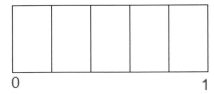

50. Write down the missing number(s) between 0 and 1:

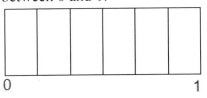

51. Write down the missing number(s) between 0 and 1:

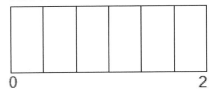

52. Write down the missing number(s) between 0 and 2:

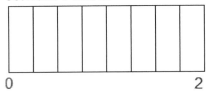

53. Write down the missing number(s) between 0 and 2:

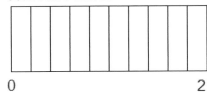

54. Write down the missing number(s) between 0 and 2:

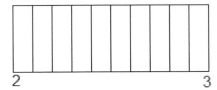

55. Write down the missing number(s) between 2 and 3:

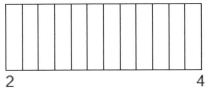

56. Write down the missing number(s) between 2 and 4:

57.   Write down the missing fractions(s) and decimal:

-5   -4   -3   ↑-2   -1   ↑   1   2   3   4   5

58.   Write down the missing fractions(s) and decimal:

-5   -4   -3   -2   ↑-1   1   2   ↑3   4   5

59.   Write down the missing fractions(s) and decimal:

-5   ↑   -4   -3   -2   -1   1   2   3   ↑   4   5

60.   Write down the missing fractions(s) and decimal:

0   [1/5]

61.   Write down the missing fractions(s) and decimal:

[1/8]   [1/2]

62.   Write down the missing fractions(s) and decimal:

[1]   [3/2]   [5/3]

63.   Write down the missing fractions(s) and decimal:

[13/7]   [2]   [20/7]

64. Write down the missing fractions(s) and decimal:

[26/9]   [3]   [10/3]

65. Write down the missing fractions(s) and decimal:

[-10/9]   [-1]   [-4/9]   [-1/3]

66. Write down the missing fractions(s) and decimal:

[-4]   [-2]   [-8/5]   [-6/5]

67. Write down the missing fractions(s) and decimal:

[3/4]   [3/2]   [9/4]   [3]   [6]   [27/4]   [15/2]

1.3. – DECIMALS AND FRACTIONS

Write the fractions as decimals:

1. $\dfrac{1}{10} =$

2. $\dfrac{1}{100} =$

3. $\dfrac{1}{1000} =$

4. $\dfrac{1}{10000} =$

5. $\dfrac{2}{10} =$

6. $\dfrac{5}{100} =$

7. $\dfrac{-31}{1000} =$

8. $\dfrac{766}{10000} =$

9. $\dfrac{55}{10} =$

10. $\dfrac{101}{100} =$

11. $\dfrac{-335}{1000} =$

12. $\dfrac{20000}{10000} =$

13. $\dfrac{1}{2} =$

14. $\dfrac{1}{5} =$

15. $\dfrac{1}{4} =$

16. $\dfrac{1}{3} =$

17. $\dfrac{1}{8} =$

18. $\dfrac{1}{9} =$

19. $\dfrac{2}{5} =$

20. $\dfrac{2}{4} =$

21. $\dfrac{3}{5} =$

22. $\dfrac{4}{5} =$

23. $\dfrac{3}{4} =$

24. $\dfrac{7}{5} =$

25. $\dfrac{5}{4} =$

26. $\dfrac{9}{5} =$

27. $\dfrac{2}{9} =$

28. $\dfrac{1}{20} =$

29. $\dfrac{3}{20} =$

30. $\dfrac{8}{5} =$

31. $\dfrac{18}{10} =$

Write the decimals as fractions:

32. $0.3 =$

33. $0.2 =$

34. $0.1 =$

35. $0.01 =$

36. $0.02 =$

37. $0.11 =$

38. $0.26 =$

39. $1.3 =$

40. $1.42 =$

41. $0.011 =$

42. $0.312 =$

43. $0.16 =$

44. $1.4 =$

45. $2.043 =$

46. $43.3 =$

47. $4.12 =$

48. $1.302 =$

49. $1.111 =$

50. $102.32 =$

51. $2.346 =$

52. Write down the fractions in different ways:

$\dfrac{1}{2} =$ $\qquad$ $\dfrac{1}{3} =$ $\qquad$ $\dfrac{1}{4} =$ $\qquad$ $\dfrac{7}{4} =$ $\qquad$ $\dfrac{2}{3} =$ $\qquad$ $\dfrac{11}{8} =$

$\dfrac{a}{b} =$ $\qquad$ $\dfrac{3a}{a} =$ $\qquad$ $\dfrac{a+2}{2+a} =$ $\qquad$ $\dfrac{x}{7x} =$ $\qquad$ $\dfrac{1+a}{a-1} =$

Fill the blank to make the fractions equal:

53. $\dfrac{a}{3} = \dfrac{\;}{6}$

54. $\dfrac{a-b}{4} = \dfrac{\;}{12}$

55. $\dfrac{a}{b} = \dfrac{\;}{2b}$

56. $\dfrac{1}{a} = \dfrac{\;}{3a}$

57. $\dfrac{1}{3} = \dfrac{\;}{\_\, a}$

58. $\dfrac{a-b}{\;} = 1$

59. $\dfrac{2-a}{\;} = \dfrac{a-2}{2}$

60. $\dfrac{2a}{b} = \dfrac{\;}{4b}$

61. $\dfrac{x^2}{2xy} = \dfrac{\;}{4y^2}$

62. $\dfrac{2a}{7x} = \dfrac{\;}{14x^2}$

Perform the operations <u>using fractions only</u>; give the answer as a decimal and fraction:

63. $50 \cdot 0.1 =$

64. $85 \cdot 0.01 =$

65. $45 \cdot 0.001 =$

66. $6 \cdot 0.0001 =$

67. $5123 \cdot 0.001 =$

68. $435 \cdot 0.01 =$

69. $15 \cdot 0.001 =$

70. $-236 \cdot 0.0001 =$

71. $1228 \cdot 0.1 =$

72. $1085 \cdot 0.01 =$

73. $4500 \cdot 0.001 =$

74. $0.16 \cdot 0.0001 =$

75. $12 \cdot 1.2 =$

76. $25 \cdot 0.22 =$

77. $2.5 \cdot 1.8 =$

78. $7.2 \cdot 8.8 =$

79. $0.15 \cdot 2.01 =$

80. $87.5 \cdot 0.2 =$

81. $31.5 \cdot 0.3 =$

82. $0.215 \cdot 1.38 =$

83. $0.5 \cdot 1.23 =$

84. $1.02 \cdot 2.5 =$

85. $31.7 \cdot 0.18 =$

86. $21.2 \cdot 1.13 =$

87. $0.42 \cdot 5.56 =$

88. $3.1 \cdot 0.642 =$

89. $13.7 \cdot 8.9 =$

90. $1.07 \cdot 0.03 =$

Perform the operations <u>using fractions only</u>; give the answer as a decimal and fraction:

91. $\dfrac{1}{0.1} =$

92. $\dfrac{5}{0.01} =$

93. $\dfrac{-56}{0.001} =$

94. $\dfrac{-2.3}{0.01} =$

95. $\dfrac{3}{0.1} =$

96. $\dfrac{0.55}{0.01} =$

97. $\dfrac{-31.6}{0.001} =$

98. $\dfrac{0.023}{0.01} =$

99. $\dfrac{15}{0.01} =$

100. $\dfrac{-215}{0.01} =$

101. $\dfrac{-45.6}{0.001} =$

102. $\dfrac{-12.3}{0.01} =$

103. $\dfrac{1}{0.02} =$

104. $\dfrac{-2}{0.03} =$

105. $\dfrac{-4.6}{0.05} =$

106. $\dfrac{-1.3}{0.06} =$

107. $\dfrac{1}{0.25} =$

108. $\dfrac{-2}{0.9} =$

109. $\dfrac{-4.1}{0.2} =$

110. $\dfrac{-1.3}{0.05} =$

111. $\dfrac{1}{0.015} =$

112. $\dfrac{-12}{0.6} =$

113. $\dfrac{-14}{0.003} =$

114. $\dfrac{-0.3}{0.02} =$

115. Write down the number that is 0.2 units on the left of −1:_____

116. Write down the number that is 0.5 units on the left of −2:_____

117. Write down the number that is 0.3 units on the right of −1:_____

118. Write down the number that is 0.4 units on the right of −2:_____

119. Write down the number that is 0.8 units on the left of −9:_____

120. Write down the number that is 0.2 units on the left of 0:_____

121. Write down the number that is 0.9 units on the right of −9:_____

122. Write down the number that is 0.2 units on the right of −5:_____

123. Write down the number that is 0.21 units on the left of −1:_____

124. Write down the number that is 0.51 units on the left of −2:_____

125. Write down the number that is 0.34 units on the right of −1:_____

126. Write down the number that is 0.06 units on the right of −10: _____

127. Write down the number that is 0.11 units on the right of −1: _____

128. Write down the number that is 0.01 units on the right of −2: _____

129. Write down the number that is 0.34 units on the right of 9: _____

130. Write down the number that is 0.06 units on the right of 10: _____

131. Write down the number that is 0.17 units on the right of −9: _____

132. Write down the number that is 0.78 units on the left of −3: _____

133. Write down the number that is 0.01 units on the left of −7: _____

134. Write down the number that is 0.02 units on the right of −1: _____

135. Write down the number that is 0.002 units on the right of −10: _____

136. Write down the number that is 0.111 units on the right of −1: _____

137. Write down the number that is 0.021 units on the right of −2: _____

138. Write down the number that is 0.4 units on the right of 9: _____

139. Write down the number that is 0.03 units on the right of 10: _____

140. Write down the number that is 0.202 units on the right of −9: _____

141. Write down numbers that are very close to 2 on its left: _____ right: _____

142. Write down numbers that are very close to 1 on its left: _____ right: _____

143. Write down numbers that are very close to 0 on its left: _____ right: _____

144. Write down numbers that are very close to −1 on its left: _____ right: _____

145. Write down numbers that are very close to −7 on its left: _____ right: _____

146. Write down numbers that are very close to −12 on its left: _____ right: _____

147. Write down numbers that are very close to −2 on its left: _____ right: _____

148. Write down numbers that are very close to −10 on its left: _____ right: _____

149. Write down numbers that are very close to 9 on its left: _____ right: _____

150. Write down numbers that are very close to 100 on its left: _____ right: _____

151. Write down 2 numbers between 3 and 3.1: _____, _____. Write the

     same numbers as fractions: _____, _____

152. Write down 2 numbers between 6.2 and 6.3: _____, _____. Write the

     same numbers as fractions: _____, _____

153. Write down 2 numbers between 6.2 and 6.21: _____, _____. Write

     the same numbers as fractions: _____, _____

154. Write down 2 numbers between –5.2 and –5.3: _____, _____. Write

     the same numbers as fractions: _____, _____

155. Write down 2 numbers between 0.25 and 0.251: _____, _____. Write

     the same numbers as fractions: _____, _____

156. Write down 2 numbers between 1.11 and 1.111: _____, _____. Write

     the same numbers as fractions: _____, _____

157. Write down 2 numbers between 0.21 and 0.22: _____, _____. Write

     the same numbers as fractions: _____, _____

158. Write down 2 numbers between 5.99 and 5.999: _____, _____. Write

     the same numbers as fractions: _____, _____

159. Write down 2 numbers between 6 and 6.01: _____, _____. Write the

     same numbers as fractions: _____, _____

160. Write the value of each position shown on the number line:

161. Write the value of each position shown on the number line:

162. Write the value of each position shown on the number line:

163. Circle the fractions that are greater than 1: $\dfrac{7}{6}, \dfrac{6}{7}, \dfrac{35}{34}, \dfrac{21}{7}, \dfrac{10001}{10000}$

164. A fraction will be greater than 1 if _____

165. Circle the fractions that are greater than 2: $\dfrac{50}{26}, \dfrac{60}{30}, \dfrac{35}{40}, \dfrac{20}{7}, \dfrac{20001}{10000}$

166. A fraction will be greater than 2 if _____

167. Circle the fractions that are greater than 5: $\dfrac{50}{10}, \dfrac{47}{9}, \dfrac{100}{6}, \dfrac{28}{3}, \dfrac{1201}{300}$

168. A fraction will be greater than 5 if _____

169. Circle the fractions that are smaller than $\dfrac{1}{2}$: $\dfrac{1}{3}, \dfrac{2}{3}, \dfrac{4}{9}, \dfrac{28}{29}, \dfrac{34}{60}, \dfrac{23}{51}, \dfrac{17}{32}, \dfrac{34}{67}$

170. A fraction will be smaller than $\dfrac{1}{2}$ if: _____

171. Circle the fractions that are smaller than $\dfrac{1}{3}$: $\dfrac{2}{7}, \dfrac{5}{9}, \dfrac{4}{11}, \dfrac{13}{29}, \dfrac{24}{75}, \dfrac{3}{11}$

172. A fraction will be smaller than $\dfrac{1}{3}$ if: _____

Fill the blank with: <,> or =, assume a, b, n are positive constants:

173. $\dfrac{1}{2} \underline{\quad} \dfrac{1}{3}$

174. $\dfrac{1}{3} \underline{\quad} \dfrac{1}{4}$

175. $\dfrac{2}{5} \underline{\quad} \dfrac{3}{7}$

176. $\dfrac{5}{8} \underline{\quad} \dfrac{7}{11}$

177. $\dfrac{12}{7} \underline{\quad} \dfrac{13}{8}$

178. $\dfrac{21}{8} \underline{\quad} \dfrac{13}{5}$

179. $\dfrac{35}{8} \underline{\quad} \dfrac{17}{4}$

180. $\dfrac{a}{b} \underline{\quad} \dfrac{a+1}{b+1}$

181. $\dfrac{a}{b-1} \underline{\quad} \dfrac{a+1}{b+1}$

182. $\dfrac{1}{n+1} \underline{\quad} \dfrac{1}{n}, n \geq 0$

183. $\dfrac{1}{n^2} \underline{\quad} \dfrac{1}{n}, n \geq 1$

184. $n^2 \underline{\quad} n, 0 \leq n \leq 1$

185. $\dfrac{1}{n^2} \underline{\quad} \dfrac{1}{n}, 0 \leq n \leq 1$

186. $\dfrac{1}{a} \underline{\quad} \dfrac{1}{b}, 0 < a < b$

187. Indicate the location of the fractions on the number line: $-\dfrac{7}{6}, -\dfrac{6}{7}, \dfrac{17}{34}, \dfrac{-1}{7}, \dfrac{10001}{5000}$

188. Indicate the location of the fractions on the number line: $-\dfrac{1}{6}, -\dfrac{8}{7}, \dfrac{20}{9}, \dfrac{-10}{20}, \dfrac{99}{50}$

189. Indicate the location of the fractions on the number line: $-\dfrac{4}{5}, -\dfrac{3}{2}, \dfrac{5}{2}, \dfrac{9}{8}, \dfrac{100}{33}$

190. Indicate the location of the fractions on the number line: $-\dfrac{7}{5}, -\dfrac{9}{3}, \dfrac{2}{3}, \dfrac{1}{10}, -\dfrac{66}{32}$

191. Indicate the location of the fractions on the number line: $-\dfrac{7}{8}, -\dfrac{6}{13}, \dfrac{11}{21}, \dfrac{-2}{17}, \dfrac{100}{501}$

192. Indicate the location of the fractions on the number line: $-\dfrac{10}{6}, -\dfrac{8}{7}, \dfrac{181}{90}, \dfrac{-102}{200}, \dfrac{189}{60}$

193. Indicate the location of the fractions on the number line: $-\dfrac{6}{5}, -\dfrac{5}{2}, \dfrac{2}{5}, \dfrac{90}{80}, \dfrac{33}{100}$

194. Indicate the location of the fractions on the number line: $-\dfrac{12}{5}, -\dfrac{6}{3}, \dfrac{11}{6}, \dfrac{11}{10}, -\dfrac{37}{12}$

195. Indicate the location of the fractions on the number line: $-\dfrac{10}{4}, -\dfrac{2}{10}, \dfrac{64}{33}, \dfrac{21}{10}, -\dfrac{3}{1}$

Calculate:

196. $1 + \dfrac{2}{3} =$

197. $\dfrac{5}{6} + \dfrac{2}{3} =$

198. $\dfrac{2}{7} - \dfrac{1}{6} =$

199. $5 \cdot \dfrac{3}{8} - \dfrac{2}{12} =$

200. $\left(\dfrac{2}{14} - \dfrac{3}{7}\right) \cdot \dfrac{2}{9} =$

201. $\left(\dfrac{7}{2} - \dfrac{4}{3}\right) \cdot \dfrac{1}{5} =$

202. $\dfrac{5}{6} + \dfrac{2}{3} - 6 \cdot \dfrac{1}{2} =$

203. $\left(\dfrac{7}{2} - \dfrac{4}{3} \cdot \dfrac{1}{5}\right) - \dfrac{1}{5} =$

204. $2 - \dfrac{3}{10} - \dfrac{4}{3} \cdot \dfrac{1}{5} =$

19

205. $4 - \left(\dfrac{5}{6} - \dfrac{4}{3} \right) \cdot \dfrac{1}{5} =$

206. $\dfrac{1}{a} + \dfrac{1}{a} =$

207. $\dfrac{1}{d} + d =$

208. $\dfrac{1}{a} + \dfrac{a}{1} =$

209. $\dfrac{1}{b+1} + b =$

210. $\dfrac{a}{b} + \dfrac{1}{b} =$

211. $\dfrac{a}{b} + \dfrac{d}{b} =$

212. $\dfrac{a}{c} + \dfrac{d}{b} =$

213. $\dfrac{a+b}{b} + \dfrac{d}{b} + 2 =$

214. $\dfrac{\left(\dfrac{a}{b} \right)}{b} =$

215. $\dfrac{a}{\left(\dfrac{a}{b} \right)} =$

216. $\dfrac{\left(\dfrac{b}{a} \right)}{b} =$

217. $\dfrac{\left(\dfrac{b}{a} \right)}{1} =$

218. $\dfrac{\left(\dfrac{1}{a} \right)}{b} =$

219. $\dfrac{\left(\dfrac{b}{1} \right)}{b} =$

220. $\dfrac{1}{\left(\dfrac{a}{b} \right)} =$

221. $\dfrac{\left(\dfrac{a}{b} \right)}{\left(\dfrac{a}{b} \right)} =$

222. $\dfrac{\left(\dfrac{b}{a} \right)}{\left(\dfrac{a}{b} \right)} =$

223. $\dfrac{\left(\dfrac{a}{1} \right)}{\left(\dfrac{a}{b} \right)} =$

224. $\dfrac{\left(\dfrac{a}{b} \right)}{\left(\dfrac{1}{b} \right)} =$

225. $\dfrac{\left(\dfrac{c+1}{d} \right)}{\left(\dfrac{1}{d} + d \right)} =$

226. $\dfrac{1}{\left(\dfrac{1}{d} + d \right)} + d =$

227. $\dfrac{1-d}{(d+2)} + \dfrac{2}{d} =$

228. $\dfrac{1}{d} + \dfrac{2}{d^2} + \dfrac{1}{d^3} =$

229. $\dfrac{2}{3} + \dfrac{3a}{c} - \dfrac{b}{2} =$

230. $\dfrac{\left(\dfrac{4}{b} - \dfrac{a}{7}\right)}{2} =$

231. $\dfrac{a}{c(c+1)} + \dfrac{d}{c+1} =$

232. $\dfrac{2x}{\left(\dfrac{2x+2}{3+x}\right)} + \dfrac{\left(\dfrac{x+1}{x-2}\right)}{x-3} =$

233. $\dfrac{\left(2x + \dfrac{1}{x}\right)}{\left(1 + \dfrac{1}{x}\right)} =$

234. $\dfrac{12}{2a} \times \dfrac{a+1}{6} =$

235. $\dfrac{12}{2a} \div \dfrac{a}{6} =$

236. $3 \times \dfrac{4}{3} =$

237. $3 \div \dfrac{4}{3} =$

238. $12 - \dfrac{4}{3} =$

239. $a \times \dfrac{b}{3c} =$

240. $\dfrac{b}{3a} \div 3a =$

241. $\dfrac{b}{3a} \times 3a =$

242. $\dfrac{\left(\dfrac{1}{3} + \dfrac{2}{5}\right)}{\left(\dfrac{5}{3} - \dfrac{1}{3}\right)} =$

243. $\dfrac{\left(\dfrac{b}{3c}\right)}{2} =$

244. $\dfrac{\left(\dfrac{1}{2}\right)}{2\left(\dfrac{2}{3c}\right)} =$

245. $\dfrac{\left(\dfrac{1}{2}\right)}{2} =$

246. $\dfrac{\left(\dfrac{2}{7}\right)}{3} =$

247. $\dfrac{2}{\left(\dfrac{2}{7}\right)} =$

248. $\dfrac{3}{\left(\dfrac{a}{7}\right)} =$

249. $\dfrac{6}{\left(\dfrac{8}{3}\right)} =$

250. $\dfrac{\left(\dfrac{4}{3}\right)}{\left(\dfrac{3}{4}\right)} =$

251. $\dfrac{\left(\dfrac{2}{3}\right)}{\left(\dfrac{4}{5}\right)} =$

252. $\dfrac{\left(\dfrac{2}{3}\right)}{\left(\dfrac{2}{3}\right)} =$

253. $\left(\dfrac{a}{b}\right) \cdot \left(\dfrac{c}{a}\right) =$

254. $\left(\dfrac{2}{c}\right) \cdot \left(\dfrac{c}{7}\right) =$

255. $\left(\dfrac{b+1}{3}\right) \cdot \left(\dfrac{2}{b}\right) =$

256. $\left(\dfrac{z+1}{z-2}\right) \cdot \left(\dfrac{4}{z+1}\right) =$

257. $\left(\dfrac{3a+6}{5}\right) \cdot \left(\dfrac{1}{a+2}\right) =$

258. $\left(\dfrac{2c-4}{c}\right) \cdot \left(\dfrac{2c}{4c-8}\right) =$

259. $\dfrac{1}{\left(\dfrac{2}{4}\right)} \cdot \left(\dfrac{2}{3}\right) =$

260. $\dfrac{\left(\dfrac{3}{4}\right)}{\left(\dfrac{a}{2}\right)} \cdot \left(\dfrac{2}{3}\right) =$

261. $\dfrac{\left(\dfrac{1}{a}\right)}{\left(\dfrac{2}{a}\right)} + 2 =$

262. $\dfrac{\left(x+\dfrac{1}{x}\right)}{\left(1-\dfrac{1}{x}\right)} =$

263. $\dfrac{\left(\dfrac{1}{1+x}+1\right)}{\left(x-\dfrac{2}{x}\right)}=$

264. $\dfrac{\left(\dfrac{x}{3}-2\right)}{\left(2-\dfrac{2+x}{3}\right)}=$

265. $\dfrac{2x}{\left(\dfrac{2}{3+x}\right)}+\dfrac{\left(\dfrac{2}{x}\right)}{x+3}=$

266. $\dfrac{a-b}{\left(1-\dfrac{a}{b}\right)}=$

267. $\dfrac{2}{(1-a)}+\dfrac{2}{a(1-a)}=$

268. $\dfrac{a}{(3+a)^2}+\dfrac{2}{(a+3)}=$

269. $\dfrac{1}{(1-x)^3}+\dfrac{2}{(1-x)^2}=$

270. $\dfrac{1}{(1-x)^3}+\dfrac{2}{x(1-x)^2}=$

271. $\dfrac{1}{(1-x)(2-x)}+\dfrac{2}{x(1-x)^2}=$

272. $\dfrac{2}{(1-x)x}+\dfrac{2}{x^2(1-x)^2}=$

273. $\dfrac{a^2+1}{a}-\dfrac{a+1}{a^2+a}=$

274. $\dfrac{a+x}{x}-\dfrac{y+1}{xy}+\dfrac{2}{y}=$

275. $\dfrac{a+x}{a-x} \div \dfrac{a+x}{x-a} =$

276. $\dfrac{a+x}{a^2-x^2} - \dfrac{a-x}{x-a} =$

277. $\left(\dfrac{2c-4}{c}\right) \div \left(\dfrac{4c^2+16}{c^2}\right) =$

278. $\left(\dfrac{6xy+2}{3y}\right) \div \left(\dfrac{3xy+1}{6y^5}\right) =$

279. $\left(\dfrac{x^2-z^2}{xyz}\right) + \left(\dfrac{z-x^2}{xy}\right) =$

True or False:

280. $\dfrac{a+b}{c} = \dfrac{a}{c} + \dfrac{b}{c}$

281. $\dfrac{a+b}{c+d} = \dfrac{a}{c} + \dfrac{b}{d}$

282. $\dfrac{a+b}{a} = 1 + \dfrac{b}{a}$

283. $\dfrac{a-b}{b-a} = -1$

284. $\dfrac{a}{c+d} = \dfrac{a}{c} + \dfrac{a}{d}$

285. $\dfrac{c-d}{d} = c$

286. $\dfrac{c-d}{d} = -1 + c$

287. $\dfrac{ab}{ad} = \dfrac{b}{d}$

288. $\dfrac{a(c-d)}{a} = c - d$

289. $\dfrac{ac-d}{c-d} = a$

290. $\dfrac{2a+d}{d-2a} = -1$

1.4. – EXPONENTS

Product:

$a^0 =$ ___ $\quad a^1 =$ ___ $\qquad a^2 =$ __$\times$__

$a^3 =$ _$\times$_$\times$_

$a^3 a^2 =$ _____ $=$ ___

$$a^m a^n = \underline{\hspace{2cm}}$$

Division:

$\dfrac{a^5}{a^3} = \dfrac{\rule{2cm}{0.4pt}}{\rule{1.5cm}{0.4pt}} = \dfrac{\rule{1cm}{0.4pt}}{\rule{0.8cm}{0.4pt}} =$ ___

$\dfrac{a^2}{a^5} = \dfrac{\rule{2cm}{0.4pt}}{\rule{1.5cm}{0.4pt}} = \dfrac{\rule{1cm}{0.4pt}}{\rule{0.8cm}{0.4pt}} =$ ___

$$\frac{a^m}{a^n} = \underline{\hspace{2cm}}$$

Power:

$(a^2)^3 =$ _____ $=$ ___

$\left(\dfrac{a^2}{b}\right)^3 = \dfrac{\rule{2cm}{0.4pt}}{\rule{1.5cm}{0.4pt}} = \dfrac{\rule{1cm}{0.4pt}}{\rule{0.8cm}{0.4pt}}$

$$(a^m)^n = \underline{\hspace{1.5cm}}$$

$$\left(\frac{a^m}{b^k}\right)^n = \frac{\rule{1.5cm}{0.4pt}}{\rule{1.5cm}{0.4pt}}$$

Radicals:

$(a^3)^{\frac{1}{2}} =$ ___ $=$ ___

$(a^4)^{\frac{1}{7}} =$ ___ $=$ ___

$$(a^m)^{\frac{1}{n}} = \underline{\hspace{1cm}} = \underline{\hspace{1cm}}$$

Exercises

Write in all possible forms and evaluate without using a calculator (follow example):

1. $4^{-1} = \dfrac{1}{4} = 0.25$

2. $10^0 =$

3. $10^1 =$

4. $10^3 =$

5. $10^{-1} =$

6. $10^{-2} =$

7. $10^{-3} =$

8. $10^{-4} =$

9. $2^0 =$

10. $2^1 =$

11. $2^{-1} =$

12. $2^{-2} =$

13. $2^{-3} =$

14. $2^{-4} =$

15. $(-1)^0 =$

16. $-1^0 =$

17. $(-1)^1 =$

18. $-1^1 =$

19. $(-1)^{-1} =$

20. $-1^2 =$

21. $(-1)^2 =$

22. $-1^2 =$

23. $(-1)^{-2} =$

24. $-1^{-2} =$

25. $(-3)^0 =$

26. $(-3)^1 =$

27. $-3^1 =$

28. $(-3)^2 =$

29. $-3^2 =$

30. $(-3)^{-1} =$

31. $-3^{-1} =$

32. $(-3)^{-2} =$

33. $-3^{-2} =$

34. $9^{\frac{1}{2}} =$

35. $4^{\frac{1}{2}} =$

36. $16^{-\frac{1}{2}} =$

37. $8^{-\frac{2}{3}} =$

38. $27^{-\frac{4}{3}} =$

39. $125^{-\frac{1}{3}} =$

40. $16^{\frac{3}{4}} =$

41. $(3^{-1})^2 =$

42. $(-8^{-3})^{\frac{2}{3}} =$

43. $(-27^{-1})^{\frac{2}{3}} =$

44. $(16^{-1})^{-\frac{3}{2}} =$

45. $\left(\dfrac{1}{2}\right)^0 =$

46. $\left(\dfrac{1}{2}\right)^1 =$

47. $\left(\dfrac{1}{2}\right)^{-1} =$

48. $\left(\dfrac{1}{2}\right)^2 =$

49. $\left(\dfrac{1}{2}\right)^{-2} =$

50. $\left(\dfrac{3}{5}\right)^0 =$

51. $\left(\dfrac{3}{4}\right)^1 =$

52. $\left(\dfrac{2}{5}\right)^{-1} =$

53. $\left(\dfrac{5}{11}\right)^2 =$

54. $\left(\dfrac{a}{b}\right)^{-1} =$

55. $\left(\dfrac{1}{b}\right)^{-1} =$

56. $b^{-1} =$

57. $\left(\dfrac{-11}{2}\right)^{-2} =$

58. $\left(\dfrac{3}{-2}\right)^1 =$

59. $\left(\dfrac{-12}{\sqrt{2}}\right)^{-1} =$

60. $\left(\dfrac{5\sqrt{2}}{11}\right)^2 =$

61. $\left(\dfrac{-2\sqrt{5}}{2}\right)^{-2} =$

62. $\left(\dfrac{3+5\sqrt{2}}{-2}\right)^2 =$

63. $\left(\dfrac{-12}{2-\sqrt{2}}\right)^{-2} =$

64. $\left(\dfrac{5+\sqrt{2}}{11}\right)^{2} =$

65. $\left(\dfrac{-2-\sqrt{5}}{2+\sqrt{2}}\right)^{-2} =$

66. $\left(\dfrac{-27}{8}\right)^{\frac{2}{3}} =$

67. $\left(\dfrac{16}{9}\right)^{\frac{3}{4}} =$

68. $\left(\dfrac{1}{2}\right)^{\frac{3}{2}} =$

69. $\left(\dfrac{9}{16}\right)^{\frac{1}{2}} =$

70. $\left(\dfrac{8}{27}\right)^{-\frac{1}{3}} =$

71. $a^{-2} =$

72. $a^{-\frac{1}{2}} =$

73. $a^{-\frac{2}{7}} =$

74. $5^{27}5^{-29} =$

75. $4^{27}2^{-49} =$

76. $9^{12}3^{-20} =$

77. $a^{7}a^{-9} =$

78. $(-125)^{\frac{2}{3}} =$

79. $\dfrac{5^{10}}{5^{2}} =$

80. $\dfrac{3^{10}}{9^{2}}3^{-2} =$

81. $\dfrac{3^{1}}{9^{\frac{1}{2}}}3^{-\frac{1}{2}} =$

82. $\dfrac{\sqrt{2}\cdot 4^{2}}{2^{\frac{3}{4}}}2^{-\frac{1}{2}} =$

83. $\dfrac{a^{-1}}{a^{-2}} =$

84. $\sqrt{\dfrac{a^{-10}}{a^{-12}}} =$

85. $\sqrt{\sqrt{a}} =$

86. $\sqrt{a\sqrt{a}} =$

87. $a\sqrt{\sqrt[3]{a}} =$

88. $\dfrac{1}{\sqrt[4]{\sqrt{a}}} =$

89. $\sqrt{\sqrt{\sqrt[7]{a^{2}}}} =$

90. $\sqrt[3]{\sqrt{a\sqrt{a^{2}}}} =$

91. $\dfrac{2\sqrt{a}}{\sqrt{2a}} =$

92. $\dfrac{\sqrt{a}}{\sqrt[3]{a}} =$

93. $\dfrac{a\sqrt{a}}{\sqrt[5]{a}} =$

94. $\dfrac{\sqrt{8}\sqrt{a}}{\sqrt{2a}} =$

95. $\sqrt{\dfrac{\sqrt{a}a^{-1}}{a\sqrt{a^{-2}}}} =$

96. $\dfrac{a}{\sqrt{2a^{-1}}} =$

97. $\dfrac{\sqrt{\dfrac{1}{a}}}{\sqrt{aa^{-2}}} =$

98. $\left(\dfrac{2}{5}\right)^3 \times \left(\dfrac{5}{3}\right)^3 =$

99. $\left(\dfrac{4}{7}\right)^2 \div \left(\dfrac{9}{7}\right)^2 =$

100. $\sqrt{\left(\dfrac{7}{5}\right)^7 \div \left(\dfrac{49}{125}\right)^3} =$

101. $\left(\dfrac{2}{5}\right)^3 \cdot \left(\dfrac{3}{5}\right)^{-4} =$

102. $\left(\dfrac{4^2}{5^{-1}}\right)^3 \cdot \left(\dfrac{25^{-1}}{64}\right)^2 =$

103. $\left(\dfrac{3^{-5}}{4^2}\right)^2 \div \left(\dfrac{9^{-2}}{2^3}\right)^3 =$

104. $\left(\dfrac{5^4}{7^{-3}}\right)^2 \div \left(\dfrac{25^{-1}}{49}\right)^{-3} =$

105. $\sqrt[3]{\left(\dfrac{3}{4}\right)^5 \div \left(\dfrac{9}{64}\right)^2} =$

106. $\left(\dfrac{2^{-3}}{3^{-2}}\right)^3 \cdot \left(\dfrac{4}{27}\right)^2 =$

107. $2^{-1} + 2 =$

108. $3^{-1} - 3^{-2} =$

109. $5^{-1} - 5^{-2} =$

110. $3^{-3} + 2^{-2} =$

111. $3^{-2} + 4^{-2} =$

112. $7^{-2} + 2^{-2} =$

113. $8^{-2} - 3^{-2} =$

114. $7^{-2} - 2^{-3} =$

115. $a^{-1} + a^{-1} =$

116. $ba^{-1} + a^{-1} =$

117. $2x^{-1} + x^{-2} =$

118. $a^{-1} - ba^{-1} =$

119. $(ba)^{-1} + a^{-1} =$

120. $\dfrac{1}{x} + x^{-2} =$

121. $ba^{-1} + (ba)^{-1} =$

122. $\dfrac{a+a}{3a} =$

123. $\dfrac{2a+a}{5\sqrt{a}} =$

124. $\dfrac{a^2 + a^3}{2a} =$

125. $\dfrac{4b^{-1}a^2}{2ba^{-1}} =$

126. $\dfrac{4b^{-3}}{\sqrt{2b}} =$

127. $\dfrac{9b^{-\frac{1}{2}}a^2}{27^{-1}b^{-1}a} =$

128. $\dfrac{4b^{-1}a^5 a^2}{8ba^{-1}} =$

129. $\dfrac{\sqrt[4]{a^2} + \sqrt{a}}{\sqrt{2a}} =$

130. $\dfrac{b\sqrt[3]{a} + ba^{\frac{1}{3}}}{a\sqrt{b}} =$

131. $\dfrac{3^{-2}}{9^{\frac{2}{3}}}27^{\frac{5}{4}} =$

132. $\dfrac{4^{-4}\sqrt{2}}{8^{-\frac{2}{3}}}16^{\frac{3}{4}} =$

133. $\sqrt{5}\,\dfrac{25^2 5^{-1}}{25^{\frac{4}{3}}}5^{\frac{1}{4}}\sqrt[3]{5} =$

134. $\dfrac{4^{-2}2^{-4}}{16^2(\sqrt[6]{16^4})}8^{\frac{1}{4}}2^{-1} =$

135. $x\sqrt{x}\sqrt{3} =$

136. $x\sqrt{x} + \sqrt{2x} =$

137. $\dfrac{1}{x\sqrt{x}} =$

138. $\dfrac{x\sqrt[3]{x}}{\sqrt{x}} =$

139. $\dfrac{\sqrt{2x}}{x\sqrt{4x}} =$

140. $\dfrac{\sqrt{3x}}{x + x^2} =$

141. $\dfrac{\sqrt{3x}}{\sqrt[3]{3x^2}} =$

142. $\dfrac{\sqrt{25x^2}}{\sqrt[3]{5x^3}} =$

143. $s^n s^{2n} s^2 =$

144. $a^{2k}ba^3 b^{2k}a =$

145. $\dfrac{3^n}{9^n}27^n =$

146. $\dfrac{3^{2n+1}}{81^{n-2}}27^{2n} =$

147. $\dfrac{6^n}{8^{2n}}24^{3n} =$

148. $\dfrac{2^n}{8^{n+1}}16^{n-2} =$

149. $\dfrac{5^{-n}}{125^{2n-2}}5^{-n+2} =$

150. $\dfrac{12^{2n+1}}{48^{3n-1}} \div 36^{4n} =$

151. $\dfrac{x^{-n}}{x^{2n-2}}x^{-n+5} =$

152. $\dfrac{2x^{-n+1}}{2^2 x^{3n+2}}x^{n+5} =$

29

153. $\dfrac{2yx^{-2n+3}}{2^5 y^{-1} x^{-4n+2}} x^{-2n+1} =$

161. $\dfrac{3^n a^{-2} b^n (a^{-2n} b^3)^{n+1}}{(9^n b^{-2n} a)^n a^{-2n} b^{n+2}} =$

154. $\dfrac{4^2 y^2 x^{-3} z}{2^2 xz^2 y^{-1} x} x^{-2} z^2 =$

162. $\dfrac{3^n + 3^{n+1}}{3^{n-1}} =$

155. $\dfrac{4^2 y^2 (x^{-2} z^2)^{-2}}{(2^2 x)^3 z^2 y^{-1} x} x^{-2} z^2 =$

163. $\dfrac{4^n + 4^{n-1}}{2^{n-2}} =$

156. $\dfrac{4^{-2} y^3 (x^{-2} z^3)^{-1}}{(2^{-3} x)^{-3} z^{-2} y^{-1} x} xz^2 =$

164. $\dfrac{7^{2n} + 7^{2n-1}}{7^{2n-2}} =$

157. $\left(\dfrac{a}{b^2}\right)^2 \div \left(\dfrac{a^{-1}}{b^3}\right)^{-3} \cdot \left(\dfrac{1}{b}\right)^3 =$

165. $\dfrac{7^{3n-1} - 7^{3n}}{7^{2n-2}} =$

158. $\left(\dfrac{ab}{b^2}\right)^{-2} \div \left(\dfrac{(2ba)^{-1}}{b^3}\right)^{-3} \cdot \left(\dfrac{2}{b}\right)^3 =$

166. $\dfrac{3^n + 3^{n+1}}{3^{n-1} + 3^n} =$

167. $\dfrac{2^n + 2^{n-1}}{2^{n-2} + 2^{n-1}} =$

159. $\dfrac{a^{-2} b^n (a^{-2n} b^3)^{-1}}{(b^{-3n} a)^3 \sqrt{a b^{-1}}} =$

168. $\dfrac{2^n - 2^{n-1} + 2^{n-2}}{2^{n-2} + 2^{n-1} - 2^n} =$

160. $\dfrac{a^{-2} b^n (a^{-2n} b^2)^n}{(b^{-3n} a)^n a^{-2n} b^n} =$

169. $\dfrac{3^n - 3^{n-3} + 3^{n-2}}{3^{n-2} - 3^{n-1} - 3^n} =$

1.5 – ALGEBRAIC EXPRESSIONS

Expand and/or Sum and simplify as much as possible:

1. $x + x =$

2. $x - 2x =$

3. $xy + xy =$

4. $3x^2 y - xy =$

5. $x^2 + x - 5x^2 =$

6. $3xy^2 + xy - x^2 y + 7xy =$

7. $x + y - (2x - 3y) =$

8. $2(x^2 y + xy) - x(2xy - 3y) =$

9. $b(ab + b) - a(b^2 - b) =$

10. $x + \dfrac{x}{2} =$

11. $a + 2(\dfrac{a}{2} - 3a) =$

12. $2(5z^2 y^3 + 3zy^3) - 2zy(6zy^2 - 8y^2) =$

13. $2(5z^2 y^3 \cdot 3zy^3) =$

14. $b \cdot ab^3 ab =$

15. $b(ab \cdot b) \cdot a(b^2) =$

16. $x \cdot ayb^6 yxb^2 =$

17. $x^m x =$

18. $a^n x^m x^t =$

19. $\sqrt{x} + \sqrt{x} =$

20. $\sqrt{x} \cdot \sqrt{x} =$

21. $x(5 + x) =$

22. $(x + 1)^2 =$

23. $(x - 1)^2 =$

24. $(x + 2)^2 =$

25. $(x - 2)^2 =$

26. $(a + b)^2 =$

27. $(a - b)^2 =$

28. $(2a + b)^2 =$

29. $(a - 3b)^2 =$

30. $(2x + 3)^2 =$

31. $(4 - x)^2 =$

32. $(x + 2)(x - 3) =$

33. $(x - 2)(x + 2) =$

34. $(3 + x)(x - 7) =$

35. $(2x + 2)(x - 5) =$

36. $(3x - 1)(x + 2) =$

37. $(x - 1)(x + 1) =$

38. $(x - 2)(x + 2) =$

39. $(x - a)(x + a) =$

40. $\sqrt{x} \cdot \sqrt{x} \cdot \sqrt{x} \cdot \sqrt{x} =$

41. $\sqrt{x} + \sqrt{x} + \sqrt{x} + \sqrt{x} =$

42. $2\sqrt{x} + 3\sqrt{x} - \sqrt{x} - \sqrt{x} =$

43. $(x - \sqrt{a})(x + \sqrt{a}) =$

44. $(x + 4)(x^2 - 4x + 3) =$

45. $(x + 6)(x^5 - 6x^2 - 3x + 1) =$

46. $(x - a)(x + 2a + b) =$

47. $(\sqrt{7} - \sqrt{x})(\sqrt{7} + \sqrt{x}) =$

48. $(ax - \sqrt{b})(ax + \sqrt{b}) =$

49. $(\sqrt{a} - \sqrt{b})(\sqrt{a} + \sqrt{b}) =$

50. $(6 - \dfrac{x}{8})(6 + \dfrac{8}{x}) =$

51. $(\dfrac{1}{x} - \dfrac{x}{8})(x + \dfrac{8}{x}) =$

52. $(\sqrt{7} - \sqrt{x})(\sqrt{7} + \dfrac{1}{\sqrt{x}}) =$

53. $(2x - 3c)(2x + 3c - 1) =$

54. $x(x + 8)^2 =$

55. $(x - 6)^2 3x =$

56. $(5 - \sqrt{ab})(5 + \sqrt{ab}) =$

57. $2 - (x + 1)^2 =$

58. $(x + 3)^2 - (x + 2)^2 =$

59. $(x - 2)^2 + (x + 2)^2 =$

60. $(x - \sqrt{2})^2 =$

61. $(x - \sqrt{2})(x + \sqrt{2}) =$

62. $5(2x - \sqrt{a})(2x + \sqrt{a}) =$

63. $(\sqrt{a} - \sqrt{b})^2 =$

64. $2(x - \sqrt{10})(x + \sqrt{10}) =$

65. $(x - \dfrac{2}{x})^2 =$

66. $(x - \dfrac{2}{\sqrt{x}})^2 =$

67. $(3x - \dfrac{2}{3\sqrt{x}})^2 =$

68. $2(\sqrt{a} - \dfrac{1}{\sqrt{a}})^2 =$

69. $(\sqrt{a} - \dfrac{1}{\sqrt{a}})(-\sqrt{a} - \dfrac{1}{\sqrt{a}}) =$

70. $(2^x + 2^{-x})^2 =$

71. $(4^{2x} + 2^{-x})^2 =$

72. $(3^{2x} + 3^{-2x})^2 =$

73. $(7^x - 7)^2 =$

74. $(a^{nx} - b^{nx})^2 =$

75. $(x^2 - y^2)(x^2 + y^2) =$

76. $(x^3 - y^3)(x^3 + y^3) =$

77. $(x^n - y^n)(x^n + y^n) =$

78. $(a^x - b^x)^2 =$

79. $(a^{mx} - a^{-mx})^2 =$

80. $(a^{mx} - a^{-mx})(a^{mx} + a^{-mx}) =$

Given the following polynomials, obtain the maximum possible common factor:

1. $x - ax =$

2. $3x - x - ax =$

3. $-x + ax =$

4. $xy + 2x =$

5. $8xy - 2y =$

6. $-6x + 12xy =$

7. $12xyz + 2xy =$

8. $14xy - 2yz =$

9. $12xz + 14xyz =$

10. $xy + 4y^2 + 5y =$

11. $z - 4z^2 + 8zy =$

12. $-8x^3 - 4xyz =$

13. $-6x^4 + x^2y^2 + x^2 =$

14. $-9x^7y^3 + 3x^3y =$

15. $-90x^{10}y^5 - 3x^3y^4 =$

16. $-80x^4y^6z^8 + 8x^{12}y^4z^6 =$

17. $xyz + 2x^2y^2z^2 + 3x^3y^3z^3 =$

18. $10x^3y^2z^4 + 2x^2y^6z^4 - 5x^2y^4z^2 =$

19. $20x^{30}y^{20}z^{40} - 2x^{20}y^{60}z^{40} - 2x^{20}y^{40}z^{20} =$

20. $ax^m + x^m =$

21. $ax^{m+1} + x^m =$

22. $ax^m + x^{m-1} =$

23. $ax^m - x =$

24. $-ax^m - x^{2m} =$

25. $z^{n+1} - z^{n+2} =$

26. $ax^{m+2} + x^{m-1} =$

Given the following polynomials factor, if possible.

1. $x^2 - 6x + 9 =$

2. $x^2 - 5x + 6 =$

3. $x^2 + 4x + 10 =$

4. $-x^2 - x + 6 =$

5. $x^2 + x - 6 =$

6. $x^2 + 5x + 6 =$

7. $-x^2 + 7x - 10 =$

8. $x^2 - 6x + 12 =$

9. $x^2 + 3x + 2 =$

10. $x^2 - x - 2 =$

11. $-x^2 + 4x =$

12. $-x^2 + 4x - 10 =$

13. $x^2 + x - 2 =$

14. $x^2 + 3x + 7 =$

15. $x^2 - 3x + 2 =$

16. $x^2 - x + 7 =$

17. $x^2 + 5x + 9 =$

18. $-x^2 - 5x + 6 =$

19. $x^2 - 2xa + a^2 =$

20. $x^2 - a^2 =$

21. $c^2 - a^2 =$

22. $x^2 - x =$

23. $2x^2 - x =$

24. $2x^2 + 3x =$

25. $x^2 + 5x =$

26. $x^2 - 7x + 12 =$

27. $2x^2 - 4x =$

28. $x^2 - 7x + 10 =$

29. $x^2 - 7x + 6 =$

30. $x^2 - x - 12 =$

31. $x^2 + x - 12 =$

32. $x^2 - 3x - 10 =$

33. $x^2 - 8x - 9 =$

34. $x^2 - 1 =$

35. $x^2 + 1 =$

36. $x^2 - 2 =$

37. $x^2 - 3 =$

38. $x^2 - 4 =$

39. $-x^2 + 1 =$

40. $-x^2 + 2 =$

41. $-x^2 + 3 =$

42. $-x^2 + 4 =$

43. $-x^2 + 13 =$

44. $-x^2 + 49 =$

45. $2x^2 - 72 =$

46. $-x^2 - 2 =$

47. $5x^2 - 125 =$

48. $-x^2 + 81 =$

49. $-3x^2 + 27 =$

50. $2x^2 - 6 =$

51. $3x^2 - 1 =$

52. $-2x^2 - 3 =$

53. $5x^2 - 6 =$

54. $4x^2 - 2 =$

55. $-8x^2 - 1 =$

56. $x^2 - b =$

57. $ax^2 - b =$

58. $-ax^2 + b =$

59. $2x^2 - 4x + 2 =$

60. $3x^2 - 3x - 18 =$

61. $-4x^2 + 20x + 24 =$

62. $7x^2 + 7x - 630 =$

63. $-5x^2 + 10x + 75 =$

64. $3x^2 - 12x - 63 =$

65. $2x^2 + 2x - 112 =$

66. $2x^2 - 12x - 14 =$

67. $-5x^2 + 15x + 90 =$

68. $-3x^2 - 12x - 12 =$

69. $-2x^2 - 26x - 84 =$

70. $6x^2 + 48x + 72 =$

Conclusion:

Factoring a quadratic expression is possible only if _____ Example: _____

If _____ both factors _____ Example: _____

If _____ Example: _____

34

Factor and simplify:

1. $\dfrac{x^2 - 6x + 9}{x^2 - 7x + 12} =$

2. $\dfrac{x^2 - 5x + 6}{x^2 + x - 6} =$

3. $\dfrac{x^2 - 9}{x^2 - 7x + 12} =$

4. $\dfrac{x^2 - 1}{x^2 - 2x + 1} =$

5. $\dfrac{x^2 - 6x + 8}{x^2 - 4x + 4} =$

6. $\dfrac{x^2 - 16}{x^2 + 5x + 4} =$

7. $\dfrac{x^2 - x - 2}{x^2 + 6x + 5} =$

8. $\dfrac{3x + 9}{x^2 - 9} =$

9. $\dfrac{x^2 - 6x}{x^2 - 7x + 6} =$

10. $\dfrac{x^2 - x}{x^2 + x - 2} =$

11. $\dfrac{x^2 - 4}{x^2 + x - 2} =$

12. $\dfrac{4 - x}{x - 4} =$

13. $\dfrac{x^2 - x}{1 - x} =$

14. $\dfrac{2x - 1}{4x^2 - 4x + 1} =$

15. $\dfrac{x^2 - 2x}{x^2 - 4} =$

16. $\dfrac{4x^2 + 4x + 1}{2x^2 + 5x + 2} =$

17. $\dfrac{3x^2 + 4x + 1}{9x^2 - 1} =$

18. $\dfrac{4x^2 + 4x - 3}{2x^2 - 13x + 15} =$

19. $\dfrac{4x^2 + 4x - 3}{2x^2 + 13x + 15} =$

20. $\dfrac{5x^2 - 12x + 4}{10x^2 + 16x - 8} =$

21. $\dfrac{3x^2 - 20x - 7}{x^2 - 9x + 14} =$

22. $\dfrac{4x^2 - 2x - 20}{x^2 - 3x + 10} =$

23. $\dfrac{2x^2 - 13x + 6}{2x^2 - 14x + 12} =$

24. $\dfrac{81x^2 + 162x + 81}{x^2 - 1} =$

25. $\dfrac{4x^2 + 11x + 6}{4x^2 + 15x + 9} =$

26. $\dfrac{4x^2 + 12x + 9}{4x^2 - 9} =$

27. $\dfrac{4x^2 - 20x + 25}{2x^2 - 15x + 25} =$

28. $\dfrac{7x^2 + 2x - 5}{x^2 - 4x - 5} =$

29. $\dfrac{2x^2 + 15x + 27}{2x^2 + 3x - 27} =$

30. $\dfrac{4x^2 + 6x + 2}{2x^2 - 2} =$

1.6. – PERCENTAGES

1. A percentage is _____ we sometimes use _____ or

   _____ to represent it.

2. Write as a fraction and as a decimal:

   a. 1% = _____   h. 0.1% = _____

   b. 10% = _____   i. 0.13% = _____

   c. 89% = _____   j. 0.06% = _____

   d. 100% = _____   k. 0.072% = _____

   e. 101% = _____   l. 1.03% = _____

   f. 110% = _____   m. 7.056% = _____

   g. 200% = _____   n. 5356% = _____

A PERCENTAGE OF A QUANTITY

3. Find (write the expression and simplify it to get a final answer):

   a. 1% of 900 = _____   i. 100% of 900 = _____

   b. 2% of 900 = _____   j. 101% of 900 = _____

   c. 3% of 900 = _____   k. 110% of 900 = _____

   d. 10% of 900 = _____   l. 120% of 900 = _____

   e. 15% of 900 = _____   m. 125% of 900 = _____

   f. 20% of 900 = _____   n. 140% of 900 = _____

   g. 25% of 900 = _____   o. 200% of 900 = _____

   h. 35% of 900 = _____   p. 300% of 900 = _____

4. Find (write the expression and simplify it to get a final answer):

   a. 1% of 50 = _____   e. 20% of 110 = _____

   b. 2% of 50 = _____   f. 25% of 350 = _____

   c. 10% of 70 = _____   g. 35% of 1100 = _____

   d. 15% of 90 = _____   h. 100% of 125 = _____

i. 101% of 520 = _____

m. 140% of 9100 = _____

j. 110% of 130 = _____

n. 200% of 240 = _____

k. 120% of 122 = _____

o. 300% of 120 = _____

l. 125% of 250 = _____

p. A% of M = _____

5. Johann scored 130 out 200 in a test, find his score in percentage?

6. Given that in a group of 20 students, 3 are taller than 188cm. Write down the percentage of student shorter than 188cm_____

7. Nina scored 70 out 80 in a test, find her score in percentage?

8. Given a square with side x. Inside it a smaller square is drawn with side length of 90% of x. Find the percentage of the area that is shaded and not shaded.

9. Given a square with length side x and a circle inscribed in it. Find the percentage of the area shaded and not shaded.

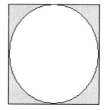

10. Given the following figure. a is 40% of x and b is 40% less of y.

    a. Find the areas of both rectangles in terms of x and y.
    b. Find the percentage of the area shaded and not shaded.

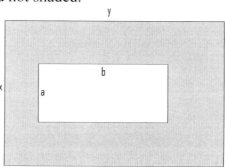

11. In a certain box of cookies there are 80 cookies of 3 colours: white, brown and black. 15% of the cookies are white, 15 cookies are brown and the rest are black.

    a. Find the percentage of brown and black cookies in the box.

    b. Dani ate 2 cookies of each colour; find the new percentages of each kind.

12. Jeff bought a car for 4000$ and sold it for 5000$, Find his benefit in percent.

13. Jessica bought a car for 4000$ and sold it for 3000$, Find her lost in percent.

14. Given the rectangle, write down the percentage of it that is shaded: _____

    Simplify the fraction:

15. Given the following square. Write down the percentage of it that is

    shaded: _____, Simplify the fraction:

16. Given the following circle, find the percentage of the circle that is shaded and not shaded. Write your answer as a fraction, decimal and percentage.

    Shaded: _____   Not Shaded: _____

17. It is known that the area shaded is 30% of 60% of the circle. Find the percentage of the circle that is shaded and not shaded. Write your answer as a fraction, decimal and percentage.

    Shaded: _____   Not Shaded: _____

18. It is known that 20% of 75% of a class of 40 students are going to the cinema. How many are going? Write your answer as a fraction and decimal.

19. It is known that 10% of 40% of a certain amount is 40 euros, find the amount.

20. It is known that 60% of 40% of a certain amount is 20 euros, find the amount.

21. Find 10% of 20% of 30% of 200: _____

22. Find 20% of 30% of 30% of 300: _____

23. Find 80% of 120% of 400: _____

24. Find 90% of 130% of 70% 500: _____

25. It is known that 20% of 20% of a certain amount is 5 euros, find the amount.

26. It is known that 10% of 30% of 5% of a certain amount is 50 euros, find the amount.

27. Given a circle with radius R cm. We know that the area shaded is 20π cm^2 and that 40% of 90% the circle is shaded. Find R in its most simplified form.

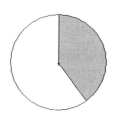

INCREASE OR DECREASE BY A PERCENTAGE

28. The price of a shirt is A $. In case the price increases by:

    a. In case the price increases by 1, state the new price in terms of A _____

    b. In case the price increases by 2%, state the new price in terms of A _____

    c. In case the price increases by 3%, state the new price in terms of A _____

    d. In case the price increases by 5%, state the new price in terms of A _____

    e. In case the price increases by 8%, state the new price in terms of A _____

    f. In case the price increases by 10%, state the new price in terms of A _____

    g. In case the price increases by 18%, state the new price in terms of A _____

    h. In case the price increases by 30%, state the new price in terms of A _____

    i. In case the price increases by 50%, state the new price in terms of A _____

    j. In case the price increases by 58%, state the new price in terms of A _____

    k. In case the price increases by 90%, state the new price in terms of A _____

    l. In case the price increases by 100%, state the new price in terms of A _____

    m. In case the price increases by 101%, state the new price in terms of A _____

    n. In case the price increases by 108%, state the new price in terms of A _____

    o. In case the price increases by 110%, state the new price in terms of A _____

    p. In case the price increases by 200%, state the new price in terms of A _____

    q. In case the price increases by 228%, state the new price in terms of A _____

    r. In case the price increases by 300%, state the new price in terms of A _____

29. The price of a shirt is A $.

    a. In case the price decreases by 1%, state the new price in terms of A _____

    b. In case the price decreases by 2%, state the new price in terms of A _____

    c. In case the price decreases by 3%, state the new price in terms of A _____

    d. In case the price decreases by 5%, state the new price in terms of A _____

e.   In case the price decreases by 8%, state the new price in terms of A _____

f.   In case the price decreases by 10%, state the new price in terms of A _____

g.   In case the price decreases by 18%, state the new price in terms of A _____

h.   In case the price decreases by 30%, state the new price in terms of A _____

i.   In case the price decreases by 50%, state the new price in terms of A _____

j.   In case the price decreases by 58%, state the new price in terms of A _____

k.   In case the price decreases by 90%, state the new price in terms of A _____

l.   In case the price decreases by 100%, state the new price in terms of A _____

m. In case the price decreases by 101%, state the new price in terms of A _____

n.   In case the price decreases by 110%, state the new price in terms of A _____

30.

a.   To increase an amount by 10% we multiply it by _____

b.   To increase an amount by 25% we multiply it by _____

c.   To increase an amount by 7.2% we multiply it by _____

d.   To decrease an amount by 12% we multiply it by _____

e.   To decrease an amount by 35% we multiply it by _____

f.   To decrease an amount by 5.1% we multiply it by _____

g.   To decrease an amount by 100% we multiply it by _____

h.   To increase an amount by 100% we multiply it by _____

i.   To increase an amount by 200% we multiply it by _____

j.   To increase an amount by M% we multiply it by _____

k.   To decrease an amount by S% we multiply it by _____

31. The price of a shirt is B $. In case the price increases by 10% and then decreases by 10% , state the new price in terms of B _____ and the overall change in the price (as a percentage).

32. The price of a shirt is C \$. In case the price increases by 20% and then decreases by 30% , state the new price in terms of C _____ and the overall change in the price (as a percentage).

33. The price of a shirt is D \$. In case the price decreases by 20% and then increases by 40% , state the new price in terms of D _____ and the overall change in the price (as a percentage).

34. The price of a shirt is E \$. In case the price decreases by 30% and then increases by 50% , state the new price in terms of E _____ and the overall change in the price (as a percentage).

35. The price of a shirt is E \$. In case the price increases every month by 4%, write the expression for the price after 80 months: _____

36. The price of a shirt is M\$. In case the price decreases every month by 12%, write the expression for the price after 10 months: _____

37. The price of a shirt is M\$. In case the price decreases every month by 2.5%, write the expression for the price after 10 months: _____

38. The price of a shirt is M\$. The price increases by x% every month. State its price in terms of M and x after n months: _____

39. Find the percentage by which:

    a. 5 is bigger than 4: _____

    b. 4 is smaller than 5: _____

    c. 11 is bigger than 10: _____

    d. 10 is smaller than 11: _____

    e. 51 is bigger than 50 : _____

    f. 40 is smaller than 45: _____

    g. A is bigger than B: _____

    h. x is smaller than y: _____

40. Given that the long side of the <u>shaded rectangle</u> is 70% of x and that its short side is 60% of y. Find the percentage of the big rectangle that is shaded.

41. Given that the side length of the square is two thirds of the short side of the rectangle find:

    a. The area of the shapes in terms of x.

        Rectangle: _____

        Square: _____

    b. The percentage of the area of the rectangle that is shaded and not shaded.

c. The percentage by which the <u>area</u> of the square is <u>smaller</u> than the <u>area</u> of the rectangle.

d. The percentage by which the <u>perimeter</u> of the square is <u>smaller</u> than the <u>perimeter</u> of the rectangle.

42. Given the diagram in which a rectangle is located inside a square. The side length of the square is 2x. The rectangle's long side is 80% of the side of the square. The short side of the rectangles is 30% less of the side of the square. Find

a. The area of the square in terms of x.

b. The side lengths of the rectangle in terms of x written as a fraction.

2x

c. The area of the rectangle written as a fraction in terms of x.

d. Using the previous parts the percentage of the area that is not shaded.

e. The percentage by which the <u>area</u> of the square is **bigger** than the <u>area</u> of the rectangle.

f. The percentage by which the <u>perimeter</u> of the rectangle is **smaller** than the <u>perimeter</u> of the square.

2. Ricardo drives to work 40% less than Rhona. Rhona drives to work 10% more than Alex who drives 400 km per week.

    a. How many km does Rhona drive to work per week?

    b. How many km does Ricardo drive to work per week?

    c. By what percentage does Ricardo drive more or less than Alex?

RATIO AND PROPORTION

43. The ratio between 2 and 5 is the same as between _____ and a 100.

44. The ratio between 3 and 7 is the same as between _____ and 35.

45. The ratio between 2 and 12 is the same as between 6 and _____

46. The ratio 1:3:7 is the same as _____

47. Divide 120 in the ratio 2:3

48. Divide 160 in the ratio 3:4

49. Divide 180 in the ratio 2:3:4

50. Divide 360 in the ratio 2:5:8

51. Divide 30 in the ratio 1:2:3

52. The diagram representing an apartment has the scale 1:50. The dimensions of a bedroom in the diagram are 5 x 8 cm. Find the dimensions, perimeter and area of the bedroom.

53. To make a chocolate cake the ingredients needed are 2 eggs, 1 cup of sugar and 3 cups of flower. Find the ingredients needed to make a cake half as big.

54. In a certain family with 2 children the parents eat twice as much as the kids. The family ordered 600g of Pasta, find the amount of pasta each one of the family members will eat.

55. The scale of a map is 1:800000. Find the real distance represented by:

   a. 1 cm

   b. 9 cm

   c. The distance in the map that represent 10km

   d. The distance in the map that represent 50km

1.7. – TYPES OF NUMBERS

Natural Numbers (N): $N = \{\_, \_\_, \_\_, \_\_, \_\_ \dots\}$

Integers (Z): $Z = \{\dots, \_\_, \_\_, \_\_, \_\_, \_\_, 0, \_\_, \_\_, \_\_, \_\_, \_\_ \dots\}$

Rational Numbers (Q): $Q = \{\dfrac{a}{b}, a, b \in Z\}$

Numbers that **can** be written as _____ being both the

numerator and the denominator _____.

Examples: $\dfrac{1}{1}, \dfrac{2}{3}, \dfrac{-7}{3}, \dfrac{4}{-1}, \dfrac{=}{\_\_}, _____, _____ \dots$

Irrational Numbers (Q'): $Q' \neq \{\dfrac{a}{b}, a, b \in Z\}$ Numbers that _____ be written as

fractions, being both the _____ and _____ Integers.

Examples: $\sqrt{2}, \sqrt{3}. \pi \dots °$

Real Numbers (R): $R = Q + Q'$ (Rationals and Irrationals)

Represented in a Venn diagram:

Fill the blanks with the corresponding letter and name

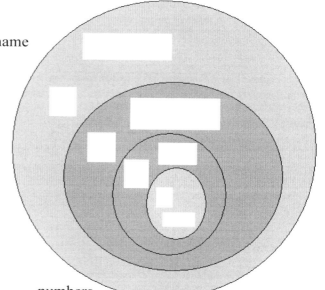

Exercises

1. Natural numbers are contained in the _____ numbers.

2. Integer numbers are contained in the _____ numbers

3. Rational numbers are contained in the _____ numbers.

4. Irrational numbers are located _____.

5. Shade the area in which the irrational numbers are located:

6. True or False:

    a. All Natural numbers are Integers: _____

    b. All Real numbers are Natural: _____

    c. All Rational numbers are Real: _____

    d. All Real numbers are Rational: _____

    e. All Integer numbers are Rational: _____

    f. All Real numbers are Irrational: _____

    g. Some Irrational numbers are Real and some are not: _____

    h. Some Irrational numbers are Integers: _____

    i. Some integers are negative: _____

    j. Some Irrationals are negative: _____

    k. Some Natural numbers are negative: _____

7. Write the value of the numbers with 10 decimal numbers (use a calculator)

    $\sqrt{2} =$ $\sqrt{3} =$

    $\sqrt{4} =$ $\sqrt{5} =$

    $\dfrac{5}{6} =$ $\dfrac{43}{27} =$

    $\dfrac{122}{90} =$ $\dfrac{158}{990} =$

    Write a conclusion: _____

8. Circle the irrational numbers:

    0.58012   0.121231234…

    0.1010010001…   0.871

    0.333…   0.227777777…

9. Fill the chart with yes or no (follow the example):

Number	Natural	Integer	Rational	Real
-2	no	yes	yes	yes
π				
$-3.121212\ldots$				
-15.16				
$\sqrt{3}$				
$-2\frac{2}{5}$				
$\sqrt[3]{8}$				
$9^{\frac{1}{3}}$				
2^{-3}				
800.0				
0				
$\frac{7}{3}$				
$-\frac{100}{50}$				
$-\frac{100}{51}$				

10. Fill the numbers column with appropriate numbers and yes or no. Follow the example.

Number	Natural	Integer	Rational	Real
	no	yes		
		no	yes	yes
	yes	yes	yes	
			no	yes
		no	yes	yes
			yes	
	no			
		yes	no	

11. If possible, convert the following numbers into the form: $\dfrac{n}{m}$

1. $0.333... =$

2. $1.151151115... =$

3. $5.3 =$

4. $5.2828... =$

5. $-2.3535... =$

6. $42.67 =$

7. $12.355355... =$

8. $-31.44 =$

9. $0.125125... =$

10. $3.22332233... =$

11. $1115.36 =$

12. $122.53 =$

13. $1.123123... =$

14. $1.22565656... =$

15. $1.5696969... =$

16. $5.540404040... =$

12. Given the following diagram:

Write the following numbers in the appropriate location in the diagram:

a. 2.2

b. -5

c. 3

d. $\dfrac{1}{3}$

e. 5^{-2}

f. $27^{-\frac{1}{3}}$

g. -3.3

h. $1.111\ldots$

i. $\dfrac{1}{\sqrt{3}}$

j. 2π

k. $1+2\pi$

l. $16^{-0.25}$

m. $\sqrt{2}+3$

n. $\dfrac{4}{2}$

o. $7^{0.5}$

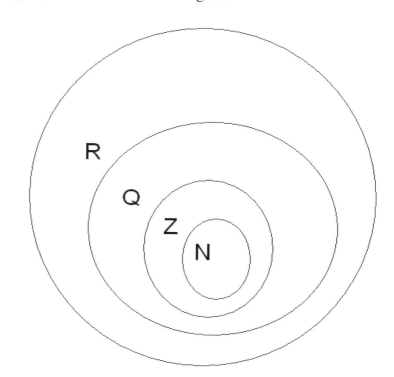

Circle the right option

13. The number -2 is:
    a. Integer and Natural.
    b. Positive
    c. Integer and Rational
    d. Natural and Real
    e. Natural and Rational
    f. None of the above

14. The number $3.41414141\ldots$ is:
    g. Integer and Natural.
    h. Natural
    i. Integer and Real
    j. Rational and Integer
    k. Rational
    l. None of the above

15. The number 3.41 is:
    m. Integer and Natural.
    n. Integer
    o. Rational and Real
    p. Integer and Real
    q. Rational and negative
    r. None of the above

16. The number $\sqrt{31}$ is:
    s. Integer and Natural.
    t. Integer
    u. Decimal
    v. Integer and Real
    w. Rational
    x. Irrational

17. The number 5 is:
    y. Natural.
    z. Integer
    aa. Real
    bb. Integer and Natural
    cc. Rational and Natural
    dd. All of the above

Simplify as much as possible:

1. $\sqrt{0} =$

2. $\sqrt{1} =$

3. $\sqrt{4} =$

4. $\sqrt[3]{8} =$

5. $\sqrt{100} =$

6. $\sqrt{81} =$

7. $\sqrt{121} =$

8. $\sqrt[3]{27} =$

9. $\sqrt{169} =$

10. $\sqrt[4]{16} =$

11. $\sqrt{10000} =$

12. $\sqrt[3]{64} =$

13. $\sqrt[3]{a^3} =$

14. $\sqrt{16} \cdot \sqrt{25} =$

15. $\sqrt[4]{2} \cdot \sqrt[4]{8} =$

16. $\sqrt{-1} =$

17. $\left(\sqrt{4}\right)^2 =$

18. $\sqrt[4]{81} =$

19. $\left(-\sqrt{5}\right)^2 \cdot \left(\sqrt[3]{3}\right)^3 =$

20. $\left(\sqrt{532}\right)^2 =$

21. $\left(\sqrt{a}\right)^2 \left(\sqrt[n]{a}\right)^n =$

22. $\sqrt{0.01} =$

23. $\sqrt{0.25} =$

24. $\sqrt{2.25} =$

25. $\sqrt{\dfrac{a^2}{9}} =$

26. $\sqrt{\dfrac{8}{200}} =$

27. $\sqrt{3} + \sqrt{3} =$

28. $\sqrt{2} + \sqrt{2} + \sqrt{2} =$

29. $\sqrt{2} + \sqrt{8} + \sqrt{2} =$

30. $\sqrt{4} + \sqrt{2} + \sqrt{8} =$

31. $\sqrt{9} + \sqrt{12} + \sqrt{27} =$

32. $\sqrt{50} + \sqrt{75} + \sqrt{12} =$

33. $\sqrt[3]{16} + \sqrt[3]{54} =$

34. $\sqrt[4]{32} - \sqrt[4]{162} =$

35. $\sqrt{27} + \sqrt{81} + \sqrt{48} =$

36. $\sqrt{200} + \sqrt{50} - \sqrt{18} =$

37. $\sqrt{20} + \sqrt{80} - \sqrt{125} =$

38. $\sqrt{10}\sqrt{10} =$

39. $\sqrt[3]{a} \cdot \sqrt[3]{a} \cdot \sqrt[3]{a} =$

40. $\sqrt{3}\sqrt{9}\sqrt{3} =$

41. $\dfrac{\sqrt{200}}{\sqrt{2}} =$

42. $\dfrac{\sqrt{72}}{\sqrt{2}} =$

43. $\dfrac{\sqrt{75}}{\sqrt{5}} =$

44. $\sqrt{3}\,\dfrac{\sqrt{24}}{\sqrt{2}} =$

45. $\sqrt{a}\sqrt{a} =$

46. $\sqrt{a} + \sqrt{a} =$

47. Write all the integers between $\sqrt{3}$ and $\sqrt{10}$: _____

48. Write all the integers between $\sqrt{13}$ and $\sqrt{50}$: _____

49. Write a rational number non - integer between $\sqrt{3}$ and $\sqrt{10}$: _____

50. Write all the integers between $\sqrt{24}$ and $\sqrt{80}$: _____

51. Write a rational number non - integer between $\sqrt{13}$ and $\sqrt{30}$: _____

Rationalize the denominator:

52. $\dfrac{1}{\sqrt{2}} =$

53. $\dfrac{3}{\sqrt{5}+1} =$

54. $\dfrac{-7}{\sqrt{5}-2} =$

55. $\dfrac{\sqrt{2}+3}{-5} =$

56. $\dfrac{\sqrt{2}+3}{\sqrt{6}-5} =$

57. $\dfrac{\sqrt{2}}{\sqrt{6}+\sqrt{3}} =$

58. $\dfrac{\sqrt{2}-1}{2\sqrt{5}-\sqrt{3}} =$

59. $\dfrac{-1}{2\sqrt{a}+b} =$

60. $\dfrac{3\sqrt{a}-2b}{2\sqrt{a}+\sqrt{b}} =$

Rationalize the numerator:

61. $\dfrac{\sqrt{4}}{\sqrt{5}} =$

62. $\dfrac{3-\sqrt{2}}{\sqrt{5}+1} =$

63. $\dfrac{-7}{\sqrt{5}-2} =$

64. $\dfrac{\sqrt{2}+3}{\sqrt{6}-5} =$

65. $\dfrac{\sqrt{2}}{\sqrt{x}+\sqrt{3}} =$

66. $\dfrac{\sqrt{b}-a}{2\sqrt{a}-\sqrt{3}} =$

67. $\dfrac{-3\sqrt{7}+8}{2\sqrt{5}+7} =$

68. $\dfrac{\sqrt{a}-2\sqrt{b}}{2\sqrt{a}+\sqrt{b}} =$

1.9. – INTERVAL NOTATION AND INEQUALITIES

x ϶ (a, b] or {x| a < x ≤ b} means x is between a and b, not including a and including b.

Exercises:

1. Represent the following Intervals on the real line:

a. x ∈ (2, 5]

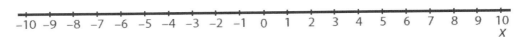

b. x ∈ (3,6)

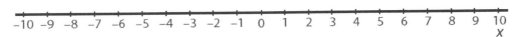

c. x ∈ [–5,9]

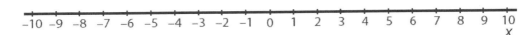

d. x ∈ [–8,–1)

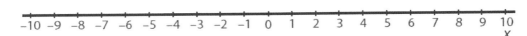

e. x ∈ [–∞,–1)

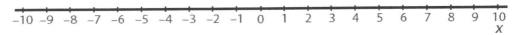

f. x ∈ [–∞,6]

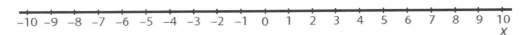

g. x ∈ (6, ∞]

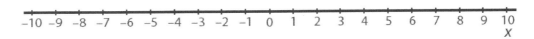

h. {x| 7 < x < 9}

i. {x| –7 < x < –2}

j. {x| 1 < x < 2}

-10 -9 -8 -7 -6 -5 -4 -3 -2 -1 0 1 2 3 4 5 6 7 8 9 10
                                                            x

k. {x| ∞ < x < 2}

-10 -9 -8 -7 -6 -5 -4 -3 -2 -1 0 1 2 3 4 5 6 7 · 8 9 10
                                                            x

l. {x| 1 < x < ∞ }

-10 -9 -8 -7 -6 -5 -4 -3 -2 -1 0 1 2 3 4 5 6 7 8 9 10
                                                            x

2. Write each one of the Intervals using all types of notations:

a. x ∈ (4, 5)

-10 -9 -8 -7 -6 -5 -4 -3 -2 -1 0 1 2 3 4 5 6 7 8 9 10
                                                            x

b. x∈ (−∞, 5)

-10 -9 -8 -7 -6 -5 -4 -3 -2 -1 0 1 2 3 4 5 6 7 8 9 10
                                                            x

c. x ∈ (4, 5)

-10 -9 -8 -7 -6 -5 -4 -3 -2 -1 0 1 2 3 4 5 6 7 8 9 10
                                                            x

d. x ∈ (3, ∞]

-10 -9 -8 -7 -6 -5 -4 -3 -2 -1 0 1 2 3 4 5 6 7 8 9 10
                                                            x

e. x ∈]−5,9]

-10 -9 -8 -7 -6 -5 -4 -3 -2 -1 0 1 2 3 4 5 6 7 8 9 10
                                                            x

f. x ∈ [−8,−1[

-10 -9 -8 -7 -6 -5 -4 -3 -2 -1 0 1 2 3 4 5 6 7 8 9 10
                                                            x

g. {x| 7 < x < 9}

-10 -9 -8 -7 -6 -5 -4 -3 -2 -1 0 1 2 3 4 5 6 7 8 9 10
                                                            x

h. {x| −7 < x < −2}

-10 -9 -8 -7 -6 -5 -4 -3 -2 -1 0 1 2 3 4 5 6 7 8 9 10
                                                            x

3. Solve the following inequalities and shade the solution on the given diagram:

a. $-x \leq 3$

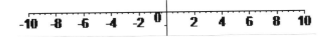

b. $5 - x \leq 2$

c. $8 - 2x \leq 3$

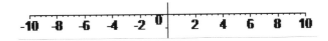

d. $-2x \leq 4 + x$

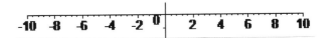

e. $7 + x \leq x + 3$

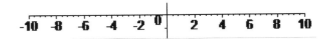

f. $-2x \leq 2x + 1$

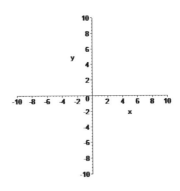

g. $-2x \leq 2x$

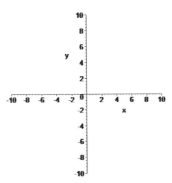

h. $-5x + 3 \le 2x - 1$

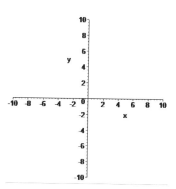

i. $7x \le 4 + 7x + 1$

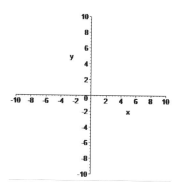

j. $\dfrac{x}{2} \le x + 1$

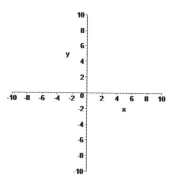

k. $\dfrac{x}{3} \le \dfrac{x}{6} + 1$

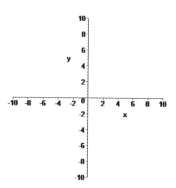

l. $\dfrac{x-4}{6} \le x-1$

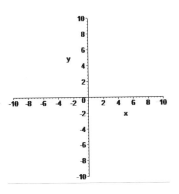

m. $\dfrac{2-x}{3} \le \dfrac{x}{5}-3$

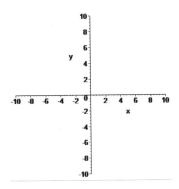

n. $\dfrac{4-2x}{5} \le \dfrac{2x}{6}-\dfrac{x}{2}$

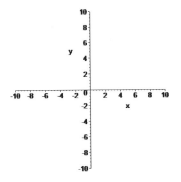

o. $\dfrac{-2x}{5}-3 \le \dfrac{x-2}{4}-\dfrac{x-1}{2}$

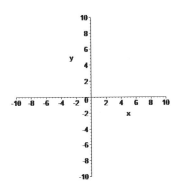

p. $\dfrac{y+4}{6} \le y-1$

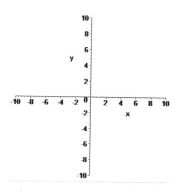

q. $\dfrac{2-2y}{3} \le \dfrac{y}{4}-1$

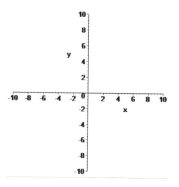

r. $\dfrac{4-y}{5} \le \dfrac{y}{2}-y$

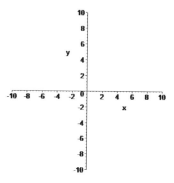

s. $\dfrac{-2y}{5}-1 \le y-\dfrac{y-1}{2}$

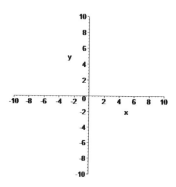

t. $-2 \leq 2x \leq 1$

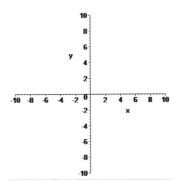

u. $-8 \leq \dfrac{-6x+3}{4} \leq 7$

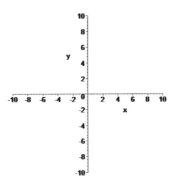

v. $-10 \leq 4y+2 \leq 9$

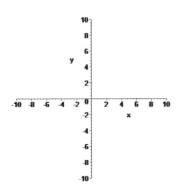

w. $0 \leq \dfrac{y+2}{3} \leq 2$

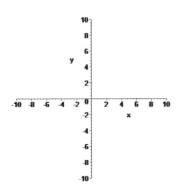

60

x. $-\dfrac{13}{5} \le -\dfrac{2x}{4} - x + 2 \le 0$

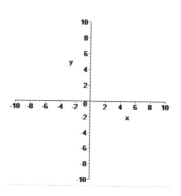

y. $0 \le 2 - \dfrac{-6x - 3}{4} \le \dfrac{13}{6}$

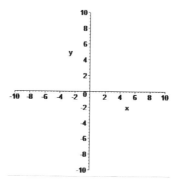

z. $-\dfrac{5}{2} \le -\dfrac{4y}{3} + y + 2 \le 3$

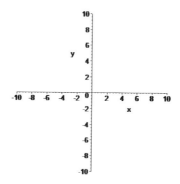

aa. $0 \le 2 - \dfrac{2y + 2}{3} + y \le \dfrac{7}{6}$

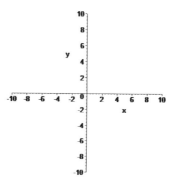

bb. $-\dfrac{12}{7} \le \dfrac{x}{2} + \dfrac{x}{3} \le 0$

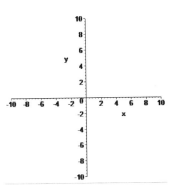

cc. $\dfrac{-7}{8} \le 2 - \dfrac{-6x+3}{4} \le \dfrac{6}{2}$

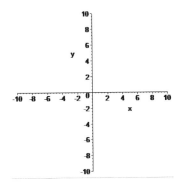

dd. $-\dfrac{10}{3} \le -\dfrac{4y+2}{5} \le \dfrac{9}{2}$

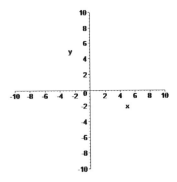

ee. $0 \le \dfrac{y+2}{3} \le \dfrac{12}{7}$

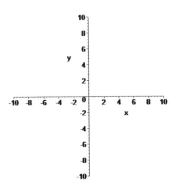

62

4.

    a. Solve the inequality $2x \leq 2$

    b. Solve the inequality $-x < -2$.

    c. Represent both solutions on the real line:

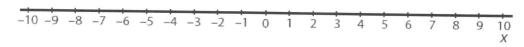

    d. State their intersection: _____ .

5.

    a. Solve the inequality $2x - 2 \leq 2$

    b. Solve the inequality $-3x + 1 > -2$.

    c. Represent both solutions on the real line:

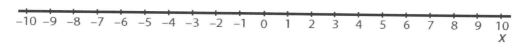

    d. State their intersection: _____ .

6.

    a. Solve the inequality $x - 2 \leq -5$

    b. Solve the inequality $-2x + 14 \leq -2$.

    c. Represent both solutions on the real line:

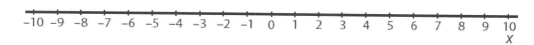

    d. State their intersection: _____

7.

   a. Solve the inequality $3x - 7 \leq 2$

   b. Solve the inequality $-x < -2$.

   c. Represent both solutions on the real line:

   d. State their intersection: _____.

8.

   a. Solve the inequality $5x - 2 \leq 2$

   b. Solve the inequality $-2x + 1 > -2$.

   c. Represent both solutions on the real line:

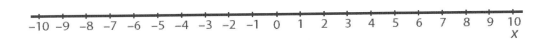

   d. State their intersection: _____.

9.

   a. Solve the inequality $5x - 2 \leq -12$

   b. Solve the inequality $-2x - 3 \leq -2$.

   c. Represent both solutions on the real line:

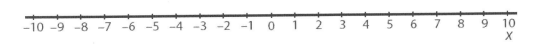

   d. State their intersection: _____

1.10. – EVALUATING EXPRESSIONS

Evaluate the expression given the value of x:

1. $x = -3$, $x^2 =$

2. $x = -3$, $-x^2 =$

3. $x = -3$, $x - x^2 =$

4. $x = -3$, $-x^3 =$

5. $x = -3$, $x^2 + x =$

6. $x = -2$, $2x^2 + 3x =$

7. $x = -2$, $x^{-1} =$

8. $x = -2$, $x^3 =$

9. $x = -3$, $x^{-3} =$

10. $x = -9$, $2x^{-2} =$

11. $x = 4$, $x^{-2} + x =$

12. $x = -2$, $2x^2 + \dfrac{x}{2} =$

13. $x = -2$, $\dfrac{1}{x} + \dfrac{x}{2} =$

14. $x = 4$, $\dfrac{1}{x-3} + \dfrac{x}{2} =$

15. $x = 10$, $\dfrac{10}{x-5} + \dfrac{x-2}{2} =$

16. $x = -1$, $5x^{-3} + 2x^{-1} + 1 =$

17. $x = 3$, $x^{-2} + x + x^2 =$

18. $x = 2$, $x^{-3} + x^{-2} + x^{-1} + x^0 =$

19. $x = 2$, $2x^{-2} \cdot x^{-1} =$

20. $x = -1$, $x^{-200} - 2x^{501} =$

21. $x = -5$, $5x^{-2} - x^2 =$

22. $x = -2$, $2^x =$

23. $x = -2$, $3^x =$

24. $x = -2$, $2^{2x+1} =$

25. $x = -1$, $2^{3x-1} =$

26. $x = 2$, $2^{\frac{3}{x}} =$

27. $x = -\dfrac{1}{2}$, $4^x =$

28. $x = -\dfrac{2}{3}$, $8^x =$

1.11. – EQUATIONS

1st Degree Equations

1. $\dfrac{x}{12} = 5$

2. $\dfrac{x}{7} + 2 = 5$

3. $\dfrac{2x}{7} + 2 = 5 - 3x$

4. $\dfrac{2x}{7} + \dfrac{2}{5} = -2x + 1$

5. $\dfrac{2x - 1}{x} = 3$

6. $\dfrac{x + 2}{2x} = 5$

7. $\dfrac{x - 2}{2x - 1} = 6$

8. $\dfrac{2x - 2}{x + 1} = -2$

9. $\dfrac{2x}{7} + 1 = \dfrac{-5x}{7}$

13. $\dfrac{-2}{x} = \dfrac{3}{x-2}$

10. $\dfrac{2x}{7} + 4 = \dfrac{3x}{2}$

14. $\dfrac{4}{x+1} = \dfrac{4}{x+2}$

15. $\dfrac{2}{x+1} = \dfrac{4}{x+2}$

11. $\dfrac{2}{x} - 3 = \dfrac{3}{2x}$

16. $-\dfrac{2}{2x+1} - 2 = \dfrac{4}{2x+1}$

12. $\dfrac{2}{x-2} - 3 = \dfrac{3}{x-2}$

17. $\dfrac{x}{2} - \dfrac{x}{5} = 3$

21. $3 - \dfrac{2x}{x-2} = 7 - \dfrac{2x+1}{x-2}$

18. $\dfrac{2}{x} + \dfrac{3}{5} = 3$

22. $\dfrac{2-x}{x-2} = 1$

19. $\dfrac{2x-7}{2} - \dfrac{3x}{5} = x$

23. $\dfrac{2-x}{x-2} = -1$

20. $1 - \dfrac{1}{x} = 7 - \dfrac{3x+1}{x}$

24. $\dfrac{5-7x}{3x-2} = -1 + \dfrac{5}{3x-2}$

25. $\dfrac{15-x}{3-x} = 7 - \dfrac{5x}{3-x}$

26. Write an equation with fractions, similar to previous one whose solution is 6, solve it.

27. Write an equation with fractions, similar to previous one whose solution is -5, solve it.

28. Write an equation with fractions, similar to previous one whose solution is $\dfrac{2}{3}$, solve it.

29. Write an equation with fractions, similar to previous one whose solution is $-\dfrac{3}{5}$, solve it.

30. Write an equation with fractions, similar to previous one whose solution is $-\dfrac{3}{7}$, solve it.

31. Write an equation with fractions, similar to previous one whose solution is $\dfrac{3}{4}$, solve it.

Isolate x

1. $\dfrac{4}{x} = \dfrac{a}{x+6}$

2. $\dfrac{14}{x+2} = \dfrac{a}{x+2} - a$

3. $\dfrac{2}{x+3} - a = \dfrac{a+b}{x+3}$

4. $\dfrac{5}{2x+1} - 3a = \dfrac{b}{2x+1}$

5. $\dfrac{-2x}{a+3} = \dfrac{x+2}{2a-1}$

6. $\dfrac{-5x+1}{2a} = \dfrac{bx}{3a+2}$

7. $\dfrac{a}{x+2} = \dfrac{b}{x+2} - b + 1$

8. $\dfrac{b}{2x-4} - 3 = \dfrac{b}{2x-4} - b + 1$

9. $\dfrac{1}{ax+2} = \dfrac{b}{x+a}$

10. $\dfrac{1}{ax+2} = \dfrac{b}{ax+2} - 3$

11. $3\dfrac{x}{ax+2}=3$

12. $-3\dfrac{2x}{ax+3}=b$

13. $\dfrac{2x-3}{2ax+5}=-3b$

14. $\dfrac{x}{ax+2}=\dfrac{2}{a}-3$

15. $\dfrac{bx}{x+2}=3-b$

16. $\dfrac{b+x}{x-3}=\dfrac{b}{x-3}+a$

17. $\dfrac{bx}{a}=2x+8$

18. $\dfrac{ax+b}{dx+2}=c-g$

19. $\dfrac{1}{x+2}+\dfrac{1}{b}=2$

20. $\dfrac{1-a}{x}+\dfrac{2a}{x}=2b$

21. $x - \dfrac{2 + ax}{b} = 2x + 3$

22. $\dfrac{7 - 2ax}{x + 1} = 2 + b$

23. $\dfrac{3 - 2x}{2x - 3} = a$

24. $\dfrac{2}{1 - x} = \dfrac{2a}{x - 1} - a$

25. $\dfrac{3}{a - 2x} = \dfrac{b}{2x - a} - c$

26. Complete the RHS of the equation so its solution is a

$$xa + 1 = \underline{\qquad}$$

27. Complete the RHS of the equation so its solution is $a - 1$

$$\dfrac{1}{xa} - a = \underline{\qquad}$$

28. Complete the RHS of the equation so its solution is $2a$

$$x - \dfrac{1}{xa} = \underline{\qquad}$$

29. Complete the RHS of the equation so its solution is $4a + 1$

$$\dfrac{x + 1}{xa} - 1 = \underline{\qquad}$$

Quadratic equations

Given the equation $2x^2 - 5x - 3 = 0$,

   1. Solve it by factoring.

   2. Solve it by completing the square.

   3. Its discriminant is _____

Given the equation: $25x^2 - 20x + 4 = 0$,

   4. Solve it by factoring.

   5. Solve it by completing the square.

   6. Its discriminant is _____

Given the equation: $4x^2 - 4x + 2 = 0$,

7. Solve it by factoring.

8. Solve it by completing the square.

9. Its discriminant is _____

Given the equation: $ax^2 + bx + c = 0$,

10. Solve it by completing the square.

11. The equation will have 2 solutions if _____ 1 solution if _____ and

   0 solutions if _____

Practice

    a. Solve the following using the "complete to square" method.
    b. Solve the following using the quadratic formula.
    c. Write the factored equation.

1. $x^2 - 4x + 1 = 3$

2. $x^2 - 4x + 1 = -3$

3. $x^2 - 4x + 1 = -13$

4. $x^2 + 6x + 2 = 2$

5. $x^2 + 6x + 2 = -10$

6. $x^2 + 8x + 3 = -10$

7. $x^2 - 12x - 2 = 3$

8. $x^2 - 2x - 5 = 3$

9. $x^2 - 3x - 5 = 3$

10. $x^2 - 4x - 5 = 3$

11. $x^2 - 3x - 3 = -3$

12. $x^2 - 3x - 4 = -1$

13. $x^2 - 7x - 5 = 3$

14. $x^2 + x - 3 = 2$

15. $x^2 - 2x + 4 = 5$

16. $x^2 + 3x - 1 = 3$

17. $x^2 + 7x - 3 = 2$

18. $x^2 + 8x = 0$

19. $x^2 - 7x =$

20. $-x^2 + 10x + 4 = -1$

21. $2x^2 - 10x - 2 = 0$

22. $3x^2 - 9x - 6 = 0$

23. $-4x^2 - 2x - 6 = 1$

24. $2x^2 - x - 1 = 2$

25. $-5x^2 + 2x - 11 = -2$

26. $-2x^2 - 2x = 0$

27. $4x^2 - 2x = 0$

28. $-2x^2 - 3 = -5$

29. $6x^2 - 7x = 0$

30. $2x^2 - 6x = 0$

31. Write a quadratic equation whose solutions are 1 and *2*

32. Write a quadratic equation whose solutions are -4 and 3

33. Write a quadratic equation whose solutions are $-\dfrac{1}{2}$ and $-\dfrac{1}{2}$

34. Write a quadratic equation whose solutions are $\dfrac{3}{7}$ and $-\dfrac{11}{2}$

35. Write a quadratic equation whose solutions are a and b

36. Write a quadratic equation whose solutions are c and 2d

3. $-\dfrac{2}{x^2 - 2x + 3} = 1$

Rational equations 2nd degree

1. $\dfrac{3}{x^2 - 4} = 2$

4. $\dfrac{x}{x^2 - 4} = 2$

2. $\dfrac{2}{x^2 - 2x + 1} = 1$

5. $\dfrac{x}{x-4} = 5$

6. $\dfrac{x^2}{x^2 - 4x} = 2$

7. $\dfrac{x^2 - 1}{x - 5} = 2$

8. $\dfrac{x}{x-4} + \dfrac{2}{x-4} = 5$

9. $\dfrac{x}{x-4} + \dfrac{2}{x+3} = -2$

10. $\dfrac{x-1}{2x-2} - \dfrac{2x-1}{x+3} = 3$

11. $\dfrac{x}{3x+2} - \dfrac{2x-1}{2x+3} = 7$

12. $\dfrac{1}{x} + \dfrac{2}{x^2} = 3$

13. $\dfrac{2}{x^3} - \dfrac{3}{x^2} = -\dfrac{1}{x}$

14. $\dfrac{1}{x-1} + \dfrac{2}{x^2 - 1} = 2$

15. $\dfrac{1}{x-3} - \dfrac{2}{x^2-9} = 4$

16. $\dfrac{5}{x-2} - \dfrac{3}{x^2-4} = -2$

17. $\dfrac{2}{x^n} - \dfrac{3}{x^{n+1}} = \dfrac{5}{x^{n+2}}$

18. $\dfrac{3}{25-x^2} - \dfrac{4}{5-x} = 1$

19. Write a rational equation that has 3 as a solution. Solve the equation to check for other solutions.

20. Write a rational equation that has $\dfrac{1}{5}$ as a solution. Solve the equation to check for other solutions.

21. Write a rational equation that has $\dfrac{2}{3}$ as a solution. Solve the equation to check for other solutions.

Radical Equations

1. $\sqrt{3} = \sqrt{x}$

2. $3 = \dfrac{1}{\sqrt{x}}$

3. $1 = \sqrt{-2x}$

4. $\sqrt{x} = 1 + x$

5. $\dfrac{\sqrt{x}}{\sqrt{6}} = \dfrac{2}{\sqrt{x+1}}$

6. $8 = \dfrac{\sqrt{2x-1}}{3}$

7. $\dfrac{\sqrt{10}}{2} = \sqrt{x^2 + 1}$

8. $2 = \sqrt{x^2 + 4x}$

9. $\sqrt{8x + 2} = 0$

10. $\sqrt{5x - 2} = 6$

11. $\sqrt{5x^2 - 2} = 3$

12. $\sqrt{x^2 + 1} = -2$

13. $\sqrt{x^2 - 2} + 4 = -2$

14. $\sqrt{2x^2 - 2} + 4x = -2$

15. $\sqrt{2x-2} + 3x + 2 = -2$

16. $\sqrt{x+1} + \sqrt{x+3} = 2$

17. $\sqrt{x-1} + \sqrt{x+3} = 2$

18. $\sqrt{x-3} + \sqrt{x+3} = 3$

19. $\sqrt{5x+1} - \sqrt{3x-3} = 2$

20. $\sqrt{8x+2} - \sqrt{3x-3} = 0$

21. $\sqrt{x-1} + \sqrt{x+2} = -2$

22. $\sqrt{x+9} = x - \sqrt{2+x}$

Higher degree simple equations

1. $x^4 - 2x^2 = 0$

2. $10(2x - 3)(x^2 - 3)(x + 5)(x^3 + 2) = 0$

3. $(2x - 3)(x - 3) = 1$

4. $(6x - 7)(3x^2 - 5)(2x + 7)(2x^5 - 64)(4x^4 + 5) = 0$

5. $3x^5 - x^2 = 0$

6. $100(x - 2)^{100}(x^2 - 5)^{10} = 0$

7. $x^6 - 32x = 0$

8. $x^6 - 2x^5 + x^4 = 0$

9. $x^3 - 4x^2 + 3x = 0$

10. $2x^3 - 5x = 0$

11. $2x^3 - x^2 = 0$

12. $ax^4 - 3x = 0$

13. $ax^5 - x^2 = 0$

14. $a(x - a)^{10}(x^2 - a)^{12}(x^3 - a)^{12} = 0$

15. $x^4 - 5x^2 + 3 = -1$

16. $x^4 - 10x^2 + 3 = -6$

17. $x^6 + 3x^3 - 10 = 0$

18. $x^8 = -2x^4 - 1$

19. $x^4 - 13x^2 + 36 = 0$

20. $x^5 - 15x^3 + 54x = 0$

21. $x^5 + x^3 - 6x = 0$

22. $x^4 = 6x^2 - 5$

Rational exponent equations

1. $x^{\frac{1}{2}} = 2$

2. $x^{-1} + x^0 = a$

3. $x^{-2} = 0$

4. $2x^{\frac{2}{3}} = 3$

5. $3x^{-\frac{1}{2}} = 2$

6. $3x^{-\frac{1}{2}} = 0$

7. $ax^{-\frac{3}{7}} = 0$

8. $3x^{-\frac{6}{7}} = -2$

9. $x + x^{-\frac{1}{2}} = 0$

10. $2x - x^{\frac{2}{5}} = 0$

11. $x^{\frac{1}{3}} + 1 = 0$

12. $3x^{\frac{1}{2}} - x^2 = 0$

13. $8x^{-2} + x^{-1} = 2$

14. $5x^{\frac{4}{3}} = -1$

15. $3x^{-\frac{3}{4}} = -2$

18. $3x^{-2} = -5$

16. $x - 2x^{\frac{2}{3}} = 0$

19. $x^{\frac{1}{2}} - 2x^{\frac{1}{6}} = 0$

20. $4x^{\frac{1}{4}} - 2x^{\frac{1}{2}} = 0$

17. $2x^2 - x^{-\frac{3}{2}} = 0$

Exponential equations

1. $2^x = 2$

6. $\left(\dfrac{1}{4}\right)^{x+2} = \dfrac{1}{16}$

2. $2^{x+2} = 2^2$

7. $2^{x+2} = \dfrac{-1}{16}$

3. $\left(\dfrac{1}{32}\right)2^{3x+4} = 4$

4. $2^{-4x+1} = 8$

8. $2^{-2x+1} = 8^x$

5. $3^{-5x+3} = 9$

9. $\left(\dfrac{1}{3}\right)^{4x^2-1} = 9^{2x}$

16. $5^{x-1} = \dfrac{1}{125}$

10. $\left(\dfrac{1}{125}\right)5^{x-1} = 1$

17. $\left(\dfrac{1}{36}\right)^{2x-3} = \dfrac{1}{6}$

11. $3^{2x-5} = \dfrac{1}{3}$

18. $6^{2x-3} = -\dfrac{3}{4}$

19. $2^x = 3$

12. $3^{2x^2-5} = \dfrac{1}{27}$

20. $2^x = 0.1$

21. $5^x = 3$

22. $4^x = 0.5$

13. $\left(\dfrac{1}{5}\right)^{x-1} = -1$

23. $4^x = 0.4$

24. $1^x = 2$

14. $5^{x-1} = 5^{x(x-1)}$

25. $2^x = -2$

26. $4^x = \left(0.5\right)^{x-2}$

15. $6^{x^2-8} = 6$

27. $1000^{2x-1} = (0.01)^{3x-2}$

28. $\dfrac{1}{5^x - 4} = 1$

29. $\dfrac{1}{5^x - 24} = 1$

30. $\dfrac{1}{5^{3x} - 24} = 1$

31. $\dfrac{2}{2^x - 7} = 2$

32. $\dfrac{125}{2^{\frac{x}{3}} - 7} = 5$

33. $6^x + 6^{x+1} = \dfrac{7}{6}$

34. $5^x + 5^{x+1} + 5^{x-1} = \dfrac{31}{5}$

35. $7^{x-1} + 7^{x-2} = \dfrac{8}{49}$

36. $7^{x-1} + 7^{x-2} = \dfrac{8}{7}$

37. $2^x + 2^{x-1} + 2^{x+2} = 11$

38. $2^x + 2^{x-1} + 2^{x+2} = 22$

39. $5^{2x} - 6 \times 5^x = -5$

40. $3^{2x} - 4 \times 3^x - 2 = -5$

41. $5^{2x} + 4 \times 5^x - 10 = -5$

42. $8^{2x} - 9 \times 8^x + 8 = 0$

43. $2 \times 8^{2x} - 18 \times 8^x + 10 = -6$

44. $3^{2x+1} - 3^{x+2} + 81 = 0$

45. $5^{2x-1} - 6 \times 5^{x-1} = -1$

46. $3^{2x+2} - 4 \times 3^{x+2} + 27 = 0$

Systems of equations

1. One equation with 1 variable may have _____ or _____ solutions. Give examples:

2. One equation with 2 two variable may have _____ or _____ or _____ solutions. Give examples:

3. Equations of the first degree are equations in which_____ Give examples with 1,2 and 3 variables:

4. Equations of the 2nd degree are equations in which_____ Give examples with 1 and 2 variables:

5. The solution to one equation of the first degree with 2 two variable, graphically speaking, is a _____. The collection of points will form a _____.

6. Write a system of equations whose only solution is $x = 1$, $y = 2$.

7. Write a system of equations whose only solution is $x = 0$, $y = -\dfrac{1}{2}$.

8. Write a system of equations whose only solution is $x = -3$, $y = -\dfrac{3}{2}$.

9. Write a system of equations whose only solution is $x = 15$, $y = -6$.

10. Write a system of equations that has no solutions

11. Write a system of equations that has infinite solutions

12. Given the equations I) 2x + y = 3, II) 2y − x = 4

    a. Write a few solutions of <u>each one</u> of the equations:

        I) (__, __), (__, __), (__, __)

        II) (__, __), (__, __), (__, __)

    b. Show the solutions on the graph.

    c. Draw a conclusion:

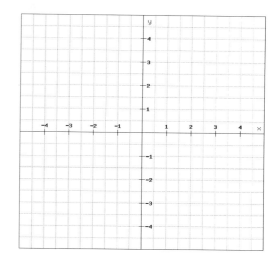

13. Given the equations I) 4x + 2y = 3, II) y + 2x = 8

    a. Write a few solutions of <u>each one</u> of the equations:

        I) _____ __

        II) _____

    b. Show the solutions on the graph.
    c. Draw a conclusion:

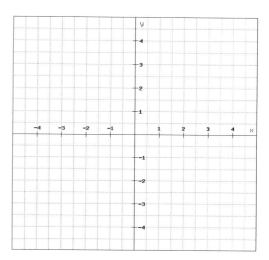

14. Given the equations I) 6x − 2y = 2, II) y − 3x = −1

    a. Write a few solutions of <u>each one</u> of the equations:

        I) _____

        II) _____

    b. Show the solutions on the graph.
    c. Draw a conclusion:

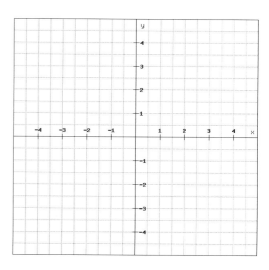

Solve:

15. $\begin{aligned} 5x + 1 &= 2y \\ 4y + x - 3 &= 0 \end{aligned}$

20. $\begin{aligned} 5x + 1 &= 2y \\ 10y - 25x &= 10 \end{aligned}$

16. $\begin{aligned} 5x + 3y &= 2 - 2y \\ -y + 2x - 5 &= 0 \end{aligned}$

21. $\begin{aligned} 2x + 1 &= 2y \\ -4y + 4x + 2 &= 0 \end{aligned}$

17. $\begin{aligned} 5x &= 2y \\ -y + 2x &= 0 \end{aligned}$

22. $\begin{aligned} x + 1 &= 2y \\ 4y - 2x - 3 &= 0 \end{aligned}$

18. $\begin{aligned} x &= 2y - 7 \\ 4y - 2x &= 0 \end{aligned}$

23. $\begin{aligned} 4x &= y \\ 3y - 12x &= 0 \end{aligned}$

19. $\begin{aligned} -5x + 1 &= 2y \\ -4y + x - 3 &= x \end{aligned}$

24. $\begin{aligned} 2x + 7y &= 4 \\ 3y - 5x - 3 &= 0 \end{aligned}$

25. $\dfrac{x}{2} - 1 = 5y$

$3y + x - 2 = 0$

28. $\dfrac{x}{5} + 2 = 4y$

$-3y + \dfrac{x}{10} + 2 = 0$

26. $\dfrac{x}{5} + 1 = 2y$

$\dfrac{y}{3} + \dfrac{x}{2} - 3 = 0$

29. $\dfrac{x}{6} + 2 = \dfrac{3y}{7}$

$\dfrac{-2y}{14} + \dfrac{x}{3} = 1$

27. $\dfrac{x}{5} + 2 = 6y$

$-3y + \dfrac{x}{10} + 1 = 0$

30. $\dfrac{x}{5} + 2 = 2y$

$-3y + \dfrac{x}{10} = -3$

31. $\begin{array}{l} x = 2y \\ -y + x^2 - 5 = 0 \end{array}$

32. $\begin{array}{l} x = 1 - y \\ -y + x^2 - 5 = 0 \end{array}$

33. $\begin{array}{l} x = 1 - y^2 \\ -y^2 + x^2 - 5 = 0 \end{array}$

34. $\begin{array}{l} -x^2 = 1 - 2y^2 \\ -y^2 + x^2 = 0 \end{array}$

35. $\begin{array}{l} x = 1 - y^2 \\ -y^2 + x^2 - 55 = 0 \end{array}$

36. $\begin{array}{l} 2x + 1 = 1 + 4y \\ -3y^2 + x^2 = 1 \end{array}$

1.12. – POLYNOMIALS

Sum, subtraction, multiplication:

1. Given the polynomials: $A = 3x + 5x^3 - 7x^{12} - 1$, $B = -3x^2 + 2x^5 - 2x^3$, $C = x^2 + x^3$
   $D = -x + 5 + 5x^4 - 4x^4 + 2x^2 - 4x^5$. Evaluate:

   a. $A + B + C + D =$

   b. $A - 2B + 3D =$

   c. $2AC =$

   d. $-3CB =$

Division: Perform the division and indicate the value of the Remainder in each case:

2. $\dfrac{x^3 + 1}{x} =$

3. Divide $-2x^3 - 5$ by $x + 1$

4. $\dfrac{2x^4 + x}{x} =$

5. $\dfrac{-2x - 5x^3 + 1}{x} =$

6. Divide $4 - x^4$ by $x - 1$

7. Divide $2x^3 + 3x - 5$ by $x - 3$

8. $\dfrac{4x^4 + x - 5}{2x - 3} =$

9. Divide $2x^3 + 4x - 7$ by $x^2 - 1$

10. Divide $5x^4 + x^3 + 2x^2 - 5$ by $-2x + 1$

11. Divide $6x^5 + 2x^4 + 2x - 5$ by $x^3 + x$

12. Divide $5x^3 + x^4 + 2x^2 - 5$ by $x^4 + 1$

13. When $x^3 - 2x + k$ is divided by $x - 2$ it leaves a remainder of 5, find k.

14. When $x^3 - 2x + k$ is divided by $x + 1$ it leaves a remainder of 0, find k.

15. When $2x^3 - x^2 + kx - 4$ is divided by $x + 2$ it leaves a remainder of 0, find k.

16. When $x^3 - x^2 + kx - 4$ is divided by $x - 1$ it leaves a remainder of 2, find k.

The Remainder Theorem

If we divide 13 by 5:

$$\frac{13}{5} = \frac{10+3}{5} = \frac{10}{5} + \frac{3}{5} = 2 + \frac{3}{5} \Rightarrow 13 = 2 \times 5 + 3$$

The same idea applies for polynomials:

$$\frac{P(Polynomial)}{D(Divisor)} = Q(quotient) + \frac{R(\mathrm{Re\,m\,a\,in\,} der)}{D(Divisor)} \quad \text{OR} \quad P = QD + R$$

Example: If we want to divide $2x^3 - 8x^2 - 6x - 36$ by x – 1 and we are <u>only interested in the remainder</u>:

$$\frac{2x^3 - 8x^2 - 6x - 36}{x-1} = Q + \frac{R}{x-1} \quad \text{OR} \quad 2x^3 - 8x^2 - 6x - 36 = Q(x-1) + R$$

Since in an equation we can do "whatever we want" as long as we do it on both sides we can substitute x = 1 on both sides and obtain:

$$2 \times 1^3 - 8 \times 1^2 - 6 \times 1 - 36 = Q(1-1) + R$$

$$-48 = R$$

Factor Theorem

In case we obtain R = 0 we conclude that the divisor is a factor of the polynomial

In each one of the following cases write the corresponding expression and use the Remainder theorem to find the remainder:

1. $2x^3 + 2x - 15$ is divided by x – 1

    $2x^3 + 2x - 15 = Q(x - 1) + R$ Substituting x = _____ on _____ sides:

    R =

2. $-4x^4 + 3x^3 - 5x + 1$ is divided by x + 2

3. $3x^3 + 2x - 4$ is divided by x + 3

4. $3x^4 + 6x^3 - 33x^2 - 36x + 108$ is divided by x – 2

5. $-2x^4 + x^3 + x^2 - 4x - 5$ is divided by $x - 2$

6. $9x^3 + 2x - 4$ is divided by $2x - 3$

7. $x^{44} + x - 5$ is divided by $x - 1$

8. $7x^4 + 14x^3 + 14x^2 + 14x + 7$ is divided by $x + 1$

9. $4x^{4455} + x^3 - x - 5$ is divided by $x + 1$

10. $2x^3 + 3x^2 - 4x - 3$ is divided by $3x - 4$

11. In which one of the questions 1 to 10 the divisor is Also a factor of the polynomial?

Factor the following polynomials and solve the equations:

12. $2x^3 + 2x^2 - 2x - 2 = 0$

13. $2x^3 + 4x^2 + 2x + 4 = 0$

14. $+ 6x + 6 + 3x^3 + 3x^2 = 0$

15. $-4x + 12 + 2x^3 - 6x^2 = 0$

16. $x^3 - 4x^2 + 4x - 1 = 0$

17. $2x^3 - x^2 - 8x + 4 = 0$

18. $5x^3 - 8x^2 - 27x + 18 = 0$

19. $-11x^2 - x + 6 + 6x^3 = 0$

20. $4x^3 - 39x + 35 = 0$

21. $5x^3 - 8x^2 - 27x + 18 = 0$

22. $9x^3 + 18x^2 - 16x - 32 = 0$

23. $x^3 - 13x - 12 = 0$

24. $9x^3 - 32 + 18x^2 - 16x = 0$

25. $3x^3 + 6x^2 - 4x - 8 = 0$

26. $x^4 - x^3 - 12x^2 - 4x + 16 = 0$

27. $x^4 + 3x^3 - 6x - 4 = 0$

28. $6x^4 + 17x^3 + 7x^2 - 8x - 4 = 0$

29. Find the values of a and b if $6x^3 + 7x^2 + ax + b$ is divisible by $(2x - 1)$ and $(x + 1)$

30. $x^3 + ax^2 - 2x + b$ has $(x + 1)$ as a factor, and leaves a remainder of 4 when divided by $(x - 3)$. Find a and b.

31. Given that $(x - 1)$ and $(x - 2)$ are factors of $6x^4 + ax^3 - 17x^2 + bx - 4 = 0$, find a and b, and ay remaining factors.

Solutions of polynomials

1. In the equation $x^2 + 3x - 10 = 0 = (x + 5)(x - 2)$ Find:

$x_1 \cdot x_2 =$ ____ $x_1 + x_2 =$ ____ $-\dfrac{b}{a} =$ ____ $\dfrac{c}{a} =$ ____

2. In the equation $2x^2 - 5x - 3 = 0 = (2x + 1)(x - 3)$ Find:

$x_1 \cdot x_2 =$ ____ $x_1 + x_2 =$ ____ $-\dfrac{b}{a} =$ ____ $\dfrac{c}{a} =$ ____

3. In the equation $6x^2 - 5x - 6 = 0 = (2x + 1)(x - 3)$ Find:

$x_1 \cdot x_2 =$ ____ $x_1 + x_2 =$ ____ $-\dfrac{b}{a} =$ ____ $\dfrac{c}{a} =$ ____

4. In the equation $x^3 - 5x^2 - 2x + 24 = 0 = (x + 2)(x - 3)(x - 4)$ Find:

$x_1 \cdot x_2 \cdot x_3 =$ _____ $x_1 + x_2 + x_3 =$ _____ $-\dfrac{b}{a} =$ ____ $\dfrac{d}{a} =$ ____

5. In the equation $12x^3 - 4x^2 - 3x + 1 = 0 = (2x + 1)(2x - 1)(3x - 1)$ Find:

$x_1 \cdot x_2 \cdot x_3 =$ _____ $x_1 + x_2 + x_3 =$ _____ $-\dfrac{b}{a} =$ ____ $\dfrac{d}{a} =$ ____

6. Conclusion:

In a polynomial _____

In a polynomial _____

$x_1 \cdot x_2 \cdot x_3 \cdot \ldots x_n =$ _____ $x_1 + x_2 + x_3 + \ldots + x_n =$ _____

1.13. – SEQUENCES AND SERIES

Given The following sequences, write the first 3 terms and the term in the 20th position. If possible identify the pattern using text (follow example):

1. $a_n = 3n$ $a_1 = 3$ $a_2 = 6$ $a_3 = 9$ $a_{20} = 60$ Pattern: ___add 3___

2. $a_n = 3n + 1$ $a_1 =$ $a_2 =$ $a_3 =$ $a_{20} =$ Pattern: _____

3. $a_n = 3n - 5$ $a_1 =$ $a_2 =$ $a_3 =$ $a_{20} =$ Pattern: _____

4. $a_n = 2n + 1$ $a_1 =$ $a_2 =$ $a_3 =$ $a_{20} =$ Pattern: _____

5. $a_n = 2n$ $a_1 =$ $a_2 =$ $a_3 =$ $a_{20} =$ Pattern: _____

6. $a_n = 2n - 4$ $a_1 =$ $a_2 =$ $a_3 =$ $a_{20} =$ Pattern: _____

7. $a_n = -4n$ $a_1 =$ $a_2 =$ $a_3 =$ $a_{20} =$ Pattern: _____

8. $a_n = -4n + 10$ $a_1 =$ $a_2 =$ $a_3 =$ $a_{20} =$ Pattern: _____

9. $a_n = -4n - 6$ $a_1 =$ $a_2 =$ $a_3 =$ $a_{20} =$ Pattern: _____

10. $a_n = \dfrac{n}{3}$ $a_1 =$ $a_2 =$ $a_3 =$ $a_{20} =$ Pattern: _____

11. $a_n = \dfrac{n}{2}$ $a_1 =$ $a_2 =$ $a_3 =$ $a_{20} =$ Pattern: _____

12. $a_n = \dfrac{2n}{5} + 1$ $a_1 =$ $a_2 =$ $a_3 =$ $a_{20} =$ Pattern: _____

13. $a_n = \dfrac{-3n}{7} + 5$ $a_1 =$ $a_2 =$ $a_3 =$ $a_{20} =$ Pattern: _____

14. $a_n = \dfrac{n}{9} - 5$ $a_1 =$ $a_2 =$ $a_3 =$ $a_{20} =$ Pattern: _____

15. $a_n = \dfrac{n}{10} - 1$ $a_1 =$ $a_2 =$ $a_3 =$ $a_{20} =$ Pattern: _____

16. $a_n = \dfrac{3n}{4} + 2$ $a_1 =$ $a_2 =$ $a_3 =$ $a_{20} =$ Pattern: _____

17. $a_n = n^2$ $a_1 =$ $a_2 =$ $a_3 =$ $a_{20} =$ Pattern: _____

18. $a_n = n^3$ $a_1 =$ $a_2 =$ $a_3 =$ $a_{20} =$ Pattern: _____

19. $a_n = 2^n$ $a_1 =$ $a_2 =$ $a_3 =$ $a_{20} =$ Pattern: _____

20. $a_n = -2^n$ $a_1 =$ $a_2 =$ $a_3 =$ $a_{20} =$ Pattern: _____

21. $a_n = 2^{-n}$ $a_1 =$ $a_2 =$ $a_3 =$ $a_{20} =$ Pattern: _____

22. $a_n = -2^{-n}$ $a_1=$ $a_2=$ $a_3=$ $a_{20}=$ Pattern: _____

23. $a_n = (-2)^n$ $a_1=$ $a_2=$ $a_3=$ $a_{20}=$ Pattern: _____

24. $a_n = 2^{n-1}$ $a_1=$ $a_2=$ $a_3=$ $a_{20}=$ Pattern: _____

25. $a_n = 2^{n+2}$ $a_1=$ $a_2=$ $a_3=$ $a_{20}=$ Pattern: _____

26. $a_n = 3 \times 2^n$ $a_1=$ $a_2=$ $a_3=$ $a_{20}=$ Pattern: _____

27. $a_n = -5 \times 2^{n-1}$ $a_1=$ $a_2=$ $a_3=$ $a_{20}=$ Pattern: _____

28. $a_n = 5 \times 2^{1-n}$ $a_1=$ $a_2=$ $a_3=$ $a_{20}=$ Pattern: _____

29. $a_n = (-3)^{2-n}$ $a_1=$ $a_2=$ $a_3=$ $a_{20}=$ Pattern: _____

30. $a_n = 2 \times (-3)^n$ $a_1=$ $a_2=$ $a_3=$ $a_{20}=$ Pattern: _____

31. $a_n = 2 \times (-5)^{n-1}$ $a_1=$ $a_2=$ $a_3=$ $a_{20}=$ Pattern: _____

32. $a_n = (-3)^{n+1}$ $a_1=$ $a_2=$ $a_3=$ $a_{20}=$ Pattern: _____

33. $a_n = 1 + 5^{n-2}$ $a_1=$ $a_2=$ $a_3=$ $a_{20}=$ Pattern: _____

34. $a_n = 3 \times 2^n$ $a_1=$ $a_2=$ $a_3=$ $a_{20}=$ Pattern: _____

35. $a_n = -5 \times 2^{n-1}$ $a_1=$ $a_2=$ $a_3=$ $a_{20}=$ Pattern: _____

36. $a_n = 2 \times 3^n$ $a_1=$ $a_2=$ $a_3=$ $a_{20}=$ Pattern: _____

37. $a_n = 5^{n-2} + 3$ $a_1=$ $a_2=$ $a_3=$ $a_{20}=$ Pattern: _____

38. $a_n = (-3)^n$ $a_1=$ $a_2=$ $a_3=$ $a_{20}=$ Pattern: _____

39. $a_n = 2 \times (-3)^n$ $a_1=$ $a_2=$ $a_3=$ $a_{20}=$ Pattern: _____

40. $a_n = 2 \times (-5)^{n-1}$ $a_1=$ $a_2=$ $a_3=$ $a_{20}=$ Pattern: _____

41. $a_n = (-3)^{n+1}$ $a_1=$ $a_2=$ $a_3=$ $a_{20}=$ Pattern: _____

42. $a_n = 1 + 5^{n-2}$ $a_1=$ $a_2=$ $a_3=$ $a_{20}=$ Pattern: _____

43. The sequences in which the pattern is add/subtract a number are called _____

44. The sequences in which the pattern is multiply/divide (pay attention that dividing by a is the same as multiplying by _____) a number are called _____

45. $a_n = 2a_{n-1}$ $a_1 = 1$ $a_2=$ $a_3=$ $a_{20}=$ Pattern: _____

46. $a_{n+2} = a_n + a_{n+1}$ $a_1 = 1$ $a_2 = 1$ $a_3=$ $a_{20}=$ Pattern: _____

47. In the last 2 sequences the terms are given in terms of _____

48. (T/F) Arithmetic and Geometric sequences are most of the sequences that exist.

49. The terms in a convergent geometric sequence tend to _____, in a none–convergent sequence the terms tend to _____ or _____.

50. Give an example of a convergent geometric sequence:

51. Give an example of a divergent geometric sequence:

52. Give an example of a alternating convergent geometric sequence:

53. Give an example of a none alternating divergent geometric sequence:

54. A convergent geometric sequence is a sequence in which r is _____.

Arithmetic sequence (Pattern – Add a constant):

General term: $a_n = a_1 + (n-1)d$

Sum: $S_n = \dfrac{n}{2}(2a_1 + (n-1)d)$

Geometric Sequence (Pattern – multiply by a constant):

General term: $a_n = a_1 r^{n-1}$

Sum: $S_n = \dfrac{a(r^n - 1)}{r - 1}$

Convergent geometric sequence $(-1 < r < 1)$: $\qquad S_\infty = \dfrac{a_1}{1 - r}$

Example:

    3, 7, 11, 15…   Arithmetic sequence.
                              Pattern: add 4.
                              General term: $a_n = 3 + (n-1)4$
                              General term can be written also like this: $a_n = -1 + 4n = 4n - 1$

Given the following sequences:

a. For each one write: arithmetic, geometric convergent, geometric divergent or neither, the <u>next term</u> and their <u>general term</u> (in case they are geometric or arithmetic only).

b. Try to write the general term of the other sequences as well.

55. 1, 2, 3, 4, ___ …

56. 1, 2, 4, 8, ___ …

57. 1, 3, 5, 7, ___ …

58. 1, 3, 9, 27, ___ …

59. 4, 6, 9, 13,5, ___ …

60. 4, 1, –2, –5, ___ …

61. 5, 0, –4, –7, ___ …

62. 10, 1000, 100000, ___ …

63. 30, 10, $\dfrac{10}{3}$, $\dfrac{10}{9}$, ___ …

64. 2, 10, 50, 250, ___ …

65. 2, 102, 202, 302, ___ …

66. 1, –1, 1, –1, ____

67. –2, 2, –2, 2, ___ ...

68. 3, –6, 12, –24, ___ ...

69. –8, 4, –2, 1, ___ ...

70. 5, 1, $\frac{1}{5}$, $\frac{1}{25}$, ___ ...

71. 100, 10, 1, $\frac{1}{10}$, ___ ..

72. $\frac{3}{4}$, $\frac{3}{8}$, $\frac{3}{16}$, ___ ...

73. 12, 11, 10, 9, ___ ...

74. $\frac{4}{9}$, $\frac{5}{9}$, $\frac{6}{9}$, ___ ...

75. 9, 8, 6, 5, 3, 2, ___ ...

76. 5, 9, 13, ___ ...

77. 1, $\frac{3}{2}$, $\frac{9}{4}$, $\frac{27}{8}$, ___ ...

78. 5, $-\frac{5}{3}$, $\frac{5}{9}$, $-\frac{5}{27}$, ___ ...

79. –1, –2, –3, ____ …

80. –2, 4, –8, ____ …

81. 70, 20, $\dfrac{40}{7}$, ____ …

82. 100, 10, 1, ____ …

83. 100, –10, 1, $\dfrac{-1}{10}$, ____ …

84. 3, 24, 192, ____ …

85. 90, 9, $\dfrac{9}{10}$, ____ …

86. $\dfrac{3}{2}$, $\dfrac{4}{3}$, $\dfrac{5}{4}$, ____ …

87. $\dfrac{40}{3}$, $\dfrac{20}{6}$, $\dfrac{10}{12}$, $\dfrac{5}{24}$, ____ …

88. $\dfrac{2}{3}$, $-\dfrac{4}{9}$, $\dfrac{8}{27}$, $-\dfrac{16}{81}$, ____ …

89. $-\dfrac{1}{2}$, $-\dfrac{1}{4}$, $-\dfrac{1}{8}$, $-\dfrac{1}{16}$, ____ …

90. $\dfrac{1}{7}$, $-\dfrac{1}{14}$, $\dfrac{1}{21}$, $-\dfrac{1}{28}$, ____ …

91. 8, 5, 3, 0, ____ ...

94. 2, –10, 50, ____ ...

92. $3, \dfrac{3}{4}, \dfrac{3}{16}$, ____ ...

95. $1, \sqrt{3}, 3, \sqrt{27}, ...$

93. $81, -9, 1, -\dfrac{1}{9}$, ____ ...

96. $7, \sqrt{7}, 1, \dfrac{1}{\sqrt{7}} ...$

In each one of the following sequences find the term indicated:

97. $1, 4, 7... (a_{31})$

101. $68, -34, 17... (a_9)$

98. $-8, -5, -2... (a_{37})$

102. $3, 14, 25... (a_9)$

99. $4, -8, 16... (a_{15})$

103. $-4000, 1000, -250,... (a_7)$

100. $32, -8, 2... (a_{11})$

104. $200, 100, 50... (a_7)$

105. The 4th term of a geometric sequence is 3, the 6th term is $\dfrac{27}{4}$.

      a. Find the ratio of the sequence.
      b. Is this sequence convergent? Explain
      c. Find a_1
      d. Find a_{12}
      e. Sum the first 15 terms.

106. The 2nd term of a arithmetic sequence is –2, the 6th term is –4.

      a. Find the difference of the sequence.
      b. Find a_1
      c. Find a_{12}
      d. Sum the first 50 terms.

107. The 10th term of a geometric sequence is 5, the 14th term is $\dfrac{80}{81}$

    a. Find the ratio of the sequence.
    b. Is this sequence convergent? Explain
    c. Find a_1
    d. Find a_7
    e. Sum the first 10 terms.
    f. Sum all the terms of the sequence.

108. The 7th term of a arithmetic sequence is 120, the 16th term is 201.

    a. Find the difference of the sequence.
    b. Find a_1
    c. Find a_{12}
    d. Sum the first 50 terms.

109. All the terms in a geometric sequence are positive. The first term is 7 and the 3rd term is 28.

     a. Find the common ratio.
     b. Find the sum of the first 14 terms.

110. The fifth term of an arithmetic sequence is –20 and the twelfth term is –44.

     a. Find the common difference.
     b. Find the first term of the sequence.
     c. Calculate the eighty–seventh term.
     d. Calculate the sum of the first 150 terms.

111. Sum the following sequences:

    a. $3 + 6 + 9 + 12 + \ldots + 69 =$

    b. $6 + 14 + 22 + 30 + \ldots + 54 =$

    c. $5 + \dfrac{5}{3} + \dfrac{5}{9} + \ldots =$

    d. $1 + 2 + 3 + 4 + \ldots + 158 =$

    e. $9 + 18 + 27 + 36 + \ldots + 900 =$

    f. $80 + 20 + 5 + \ldots$

g. $100 + 97 + 94 + \ldots + 19 =$

h. $18 + 6 + 2 + \ldots \; =$

i. $\dfrac{2}{5} + \dfrac{6}{10} + \dfrac{18}{20} + \ldots + \dfrac{243}{80}$

j. $\dfrac{1}{3} + \dfrac{2}{9} + \dfrac{4}{27} + \ldots =$

k. $12 + 7 + 2 + \ldots - 98 =$

l. $100 + 150 + 200 + \ldots + 1000 =$

112. Consider the arithmetic series –6 + 1 + 8 + 15 + …

Find the least number of terms so that the sum of the series is greater than 10000.

113. In a theatre there are 20 seats in the first row, 23 in the 2nd, 26 in the 3rd etc. There are 40 rows in the theatre. Find the total number of seats available.

114. A ball bounces on the floor. It is released from a height of 160 cm. After the 1st bounce it reaches a height of 120 cm and 90 cm after the 2nd. If the patterns continue find:

    a. The height the ball will reach after the 6th bounce.

    b. The total distance the ball passed after a long period o time.

115. In a certain forest the current population of rabbits is 200 objects. It is know that the population increases by 20% every year.

    a. Find the population of rabbits after a year.

    b. Find the population of rabbits after 2 years.

    c. What kind of a sequence is it? State the expression for the population after n years.

    d. Find the total number of rabbits after 10 years (assuming none has died).

116. In a research it was observed that the number of defective products produced by a machine per year decreases by 10% every year (due to technological improvements). In a certain year the machine made 300 products.

    a. Find the number of defective products produced a year later.
    b. Find the number of defective products produced 2 years later.
    c. What kind of a sequence is it? State the expression for the number of errors committed after n years.
    d. Find the total number of bad products produced in the first 8 years.

117. In a certain company the pay scale follows a pattern of an arithmetic sequence (every year). This means:

    a. The salary increases by a certain % every year (True/False), explain.

    b. The salary increases by a certain amount every year (True/False), explain

118. Given the sequence: $a, a^2, a^3 ...$

    a. This is a _____ sequence.
    b. Write down its general term, simplified.
    c. It is known that the infinite sequence adds up to 10, find a.

119. Given the sequence: $a^{-2}, a^{-3}, a^{-4} ...$

    a. This is a _____ sequence.
    b. Write down its general term, simplified.
    c. It is known that the infinite sequence adds up to $\dfrac{1}{2}$, find a.

COMPOUND INTEREST

1. 1200$ are put in account that gives 2% per year. Calculate the amount of money in the account after:

   a. 1 year.

   b. 2 years.

2. To increase an amount A by 5% it should be multiplied by _____.

3. To increase an amount A by 56% it should be multiplied by _____.

4. To decrease an amount A by 5% it should be multiplied by _____.

5. To increase an amount A by 15% it should be multiplied by _____.

6. To decrease an amount A by 12% it should be multiplied by _____.

7. To increase an amount A by 230% it should be multiplied by _____.

8. 1000$ are put in account that takes 5% commission per year. Calculate the amount of money in the account after:

   a. 1 year.

   b. 2 years.

9. 2000\$ are being put in a deposit that pays 5% (per year).

a. Fill the table:

Number of Years	Interest earned at the end of the year	Amount in deposit (\$)
0		2000
1	$\dfrac{5}{100}2000 = 100$	2100
2	$\dfrac{5}{100}2100 = 105$	2205
3	$\dfrac{5}{100}2205 = 110.25$	
4		
5		

b. Observe the numbers in the compound interest column: 2000, 2100, 2205… What kind of a sequence is that? Write its general term.

c. How much money will be in the account after 20 years?

d. Discuss the meaning of writing $a_n = a_1 r^{n-1}$ or writing $a_n = a_0 r^n$. Use the exercise as an example.

10. A loan of 1200$ is made at 12% per year compounded semiannually, over 5 years the debt will grow to:

   a. $\$1200(1 + 0.12)^5$
   b. $\$1200(1 + 0.06)^{10}$
   c. $\$1200(1 + 0.6)^{10}$
   d. $\$1200(1 + 0.06)^5$
   e. $\$1200(1 + 0.12)^{10}$

11. A loan of 23200$ is made at 7% per year compounded quarterly, over 6 years the debt will grow to:

   a. $\$23200(1 + 0.7)^{24}$
   b. $\$23200(1 + 0.07)^6$
   c. $\$23200(1 + 0.7)^{24}$
   d. $\$23200(1 + 0.07)^{24}$
   e. $\$23200(1 + 0.07)^{12}$

12. A loan of 20$ is made at 14% per year compounded monthly, over 8 years the debt will grow to:

   a. $\$20(1 + 0.14)^{80}$
   b. $\$20(1 + 0.01)^{96}$
   c. $\$20(1 + 0.014)^{96}$
   d. $\$20(1 + 0.01)^{12}$
   e. $\$20(1 + 0.07)^{12}$

13. A loan of X$ is made at 8% per year compounded every 4 months, over 5 years the debt will grow to:

   a. $\$X(1 + 0.08)^4$
   b. $\$X(1 + 0.02)^5$
   c. $\$X(1 + 0.08)^{15}$
   d. $\$X(1 + 0.02)^{15}$
   e. $\$X(1 + 0.8)^{15}$

14. A loan of X$ is made at i% per year compounded every m months, over n years the debt will grow to:

$$Debt = \underline{\quad}(1 + \underline{\quad})^{\underline{\quad}}$$

15. Calculate the total amount owing after two years on a loan of 1500$ if the interest rate is 11% compounded

      a. Annually

      b. Semiannually

      c. Quarterly

      d. Monthly

16. How much will a client have to repay on a loan of 800$ after 2 years, if the 12% interest is compounded annually.

17. Find the compound interest **<u>earned</u>** by the deposit. Round to the nearest cent. $3000 at 12% compounded semiannually for 10 years

18. How many years will it take to a 100$ to double assuming interest rate is 6%. Compounded semiannually.

19. How many years will it take to a X$ to triple assuming interest rate is 7%. Compounded quarterly

20. Find the interest rate given to a certain person in case he made a deposit of 1000$ and obtained 1200$ after 3 years, compounded monthly.

21. Find the interest rate given to a certain person in case he made a deposit of 2500$ and obtained 3000$ after 10 years, compounded yearly.

SIGMA NOTATION

1. The sum $\displaystyle\sum_{k=2}^{4} 2^k$ is equal to which of the following?

    a. $2^1 + 2^2 + 2^3 + 2^4$
    b. $2^2 + 2^4$
    c. $2^2 + 3^3 + 4^4$
    d. $2^2 + 2^3 + 2^4$

2. The sum $\displaystyle\frac{1}{4}\sum_{m=2}^{4} x_m$ is equal to which of the following?

    a. $\dfrac{1}{4}x_2 + \dfrac{1}{4}x_3 + \dfrac{1}{4}x_4$

    b. $\dfrac{1}{4}x_2 + x_3 + x_4$

    c. $\dfrac{1}{2}x_2 + \dfrac{1}{3}x_3 + \dfrac{1}{4}x_4$

    d. $\dfrac{1}{4}(2+3+4)$

3. The sum $\displaystyle\sum_{j=4}^{n} \frac{j}{j+1}$ is equal to which of the following?

    a. $\dfrac{1}{2} + \dfrac{3}{4} + \dfrac{5}{6} + \ldots + \dfrac{n}{n+1}$

    b. $\dfrac{1}{2} + \dfrac{2}{3} + \dfrac{3}{4} + \ldots + \dfrac{n}{n+1}$

    c. $\dfrac{4}{5} + \dfrac{5}{6} + \dfrac{6}{7} + \ldots + \dfrac{n}{n+1}$

    d. $\dfrac{4}{5} + \dfrac{5}{6} + \dfrac{6}{7} + \ldots + \dfrac{n+4}{n+5}$

4. Write out fully what is meant by

    a. $\displaystyle\sum_{i=4}^{i=6} 2i - 1 =$

    b. $\displaystyle\sum_{i=2}^{i=5} \frac{i}{i^2+1} =$

    c. $\displaystyle\sum_{i=4}^{i=6} (2i-3)^2 =$

    d. $\displaystyle\sum_{k=3}^{i=7} (2^k + \sqrt{k}) =$

    e. $\displaystyle\sum_{i=1}^{i=4} (-1)^i \times 3^{2i}$

5. Write each series using sigma notation:

    a. $4 + 9 + 16 + 25 + 36 + 49 + 64 + 81 = \sum\limits_{i=\_}^{i=\overline{\quad}}$ _____

    b. $5 + 9 + 13 + 17 + 21 + 25 + 29 + 33\ldots = \sum\limits_{i=\_}^{i=\overline{\quad}}$ _____

    c. $1 - \dfrac{1}{3} + \dfrac{1}{9} - \dfrac{1}{27} + \dfrac{1}{81} - \dfrac{1}{243} = \sum\limits_{i=\_}^{i=\overline{\quad}}$ _____

6. Use sigma notation to represent $3 + 6 + 9 + 12 + \ldots$ for 28 terms. Sum the terms.

$$\sum\limits_{i=\_}^{i=\overline{\quad}}$$ _____

7. Use sigma notation to represent $-3 + 6 - 12 + 24 - 48 + \ldots$ for 35 terms. Sum the terms.

$$\sum\limits_{i=\_}^{i=\overline{\quad}}$$ _____

8. Use sigma notation to represent: $8.3 + 8.1 + 7.9 + 7.7 + \ldots + 0.9$. Sum the terms

$$\sum\limits_{i=\_}^{i=\overline{\quad}}$$ _____

9. Use sigma notation to represent: $12 + 9 + 3 + \ldots -120$. Sum the terms

$$\sum\limits_{i=\_}^{i=\overline{\quad}}$$ _____

10. An infinite geometric series is given by $\sum_{i=1}^{\infty} 2(1-x)^i$

    a. Find the value of x for which the series has a finite sum

    b. When x = 0.5, find the minimum number of terms needed to give a sum which is greater than 1.9

11. Given the sequence x, x^2, x^3…

    a. Use sigma notation to represent the sum of its first 10 terms.

    b. Assuming its infinite and that its sum is 5 find x and write down the first three terms of the sequence.

1.14. – EQUATIONS/INEQUALITIES WITH ABSOLUTE VALUE

1. $|-3| =$ $\qquad$ $|3| =$ $\qquad$ $|-3+3| =$ $\qquad$ $|-3-3| =$

2. $|-3| + 3 =$ $\qquad$ $|3| - 4 =$ $\qquad$ $|-3+5| + 2 =$ $\qquad$ $|-3-3| - 3 =$

3. $\left| 1 - 3 + |-2| \right| =$

4. $|-2-3| + |-2| =$

5. $|-2-23| - |-12| =$

6. $2\left| 1 - 3 + |-2| + 1 \right| - 2 =$

7. $|-2-3| \, |-2| =$

8. $-|-12-3| - |-2-1| =$

9. $5 - \left| 12 - 3 + |1-2| \right| - |-12-10| + 1 =$

10. $\left| 2 - |-12-3| - |-2-1| \right| =$

11. $|x| - 2|x| =$

12. $|x| \, |x| =$

13. An absolute value of a number represents its _____

14. $|x| = |-x|$ $\qquad$ True / False, if false write down an example to show it

15. $|x+y| = |x| + |y|$ $\qquad$ True / False, if false write down an example to show it

16. $-|x|$ is _____ number

17. If $x = |x|$ it means x is _____

18. If $x = -|x|$ it means x is _____

19. If x is a negative number than $-x = |x|$ $\qquad$ True / False

20. If x is a positive number than $x = |x|$ $\qquad$ True / False

126

Assuming $a \geq 0$ the following is satisfied:

I. |x| = *a* $\qquad$ $x = a$ $\quad$ OR $\quad$ $x = -a$

II. |x| > *a* $\qquad$ $x > a$ $\quad$ OR $\quad$ $x < -a$ equivalent to $x \in (-\infty, -a) \cup (a, \infty)$

III. |x| < *a* $\qquad$ $-a < x < a$ equivalent to $x > -a$ and $x < a$ equivalent to $x \in (-a, a)$

1. $|2x| = 5$

2. $|x| = 7$

3. $|4x| = 8$

4. $|x| = -5$

5. $|2x| = 0$

6. $|2x| = -1$

7. $|2x| = 15$

8. $|2x| < 5$

9. $|x| > 7$

10. $|4x| < 8$

11. $|x| < -5$

12. $|3x| < 0$

13. $|6x| > -1$

14. $|5x| > 0$

15. $|3x| \leq 6$

16. $|x| \geq 7$

17. $|4x| \leq 2$

18. $|x| \leq -5$

19. $|2x| < 0$

20. $|2x| \geq -1$

21. $|x| \geq 0$

22. $|2+x| = 5$

23. $|-x| = 7$

24. $|4 - x| = 8$

25. $|3 - 2x| = -5$

26. $|2 - 3x| = 0$

27. $|2 + x| = -1$

28. $|2x + 3| = 15$

29. $|4 - 2x| < 5$

30. $|-x| > 7$

31. $|4 + 2x| < 8$

32. $|x| < -5$

33. $|3 + x| < 0$

34. $|6 - 2x| > -1$

35. $|5 + x| > 0$

36. $|1 - 3x| \leq 6$

37. $|1 + x| \geq 7$

38. $|4 + x| \leq 2$

39. $|3 + 2x| \leq -5$

40. $|2 + 3x| < 0$

41. $|7 - 6x| \geq -1$

42. $|1 - x| \geq 0$

43. $|2x + 1| + 3 = 5$

44. $|7x + 21| - 5 = -5$

45. $2 - |5 - 8x| = 15$

46. $|4x + 2| = -5$

47. $|8x + 12| = 100$

48. $|2x + 1| < 2$

49. $|8 - 2x + 1| > 6$

50. $|5x - 21| + 3 > 0$

51. $|5x - 21| \geq 0$

52. $|8x + 11| - 1 > -2$

53. $|91x + 61| < -2$

54. $|8 - 3x| > 8$

55. $|18 - 6x| + 1 > 3$

56. $|1 - 6x| - 2 < 7$

57. $|8 - 5x| \leq 0$

58. $|5x - 21| > 1$

59. $|x + 11| + 1 = 5$

60. $|x + 3| - 2 \leq 5$

61. $|x + 11| = -15$

62. $|2x + 11| + 2 < 1$

63. $|3x + 11| = x$

72. $|2x - 6| \geq 4$

64. $|x + 2| = 5 - x$

73. $|3x - 6| + 1 > -4$

65. $|3x + 1| < 5x$

74. $|4x - 6| - 4 < -4x$

66. $|x - 4| = 3x$

75. $|\frac{1}{2}x - 4| \leq 1 + x$

67. $|2x - 6| \leq 5 + 2x$

76. $|2x + \frac{1}{2}| > 2 - 3x$

68. $|2x + 4| < 2 - 3x$

77. $|2x - \frac{1}{2}| = 1 - 2x$

69. $|2x - 2| > 11 - 2x$

$x \in (\frac{3}{8}, \infty)$

70. $|7x - 16| = 5 + 12x$

78. $|\frac{1}{2}x - 7| \leq 3 + 2x$

71. $|2x - 6| = 21$

79. $|\frac{x}{2} + 2| = 1 - x$ $x = -\frac{2}{3}$

CHAPTER 2 - GEOMETRY

2.1. – INTRODUCTION TO GEOMETRY

POINTS

1. Indicate the following points on the plane: A(1,5), B(–1, 4), C(–3, –7), D(6,–5), E(–1, –1), F(2, 0),G(0,–4), H(–4, 0)

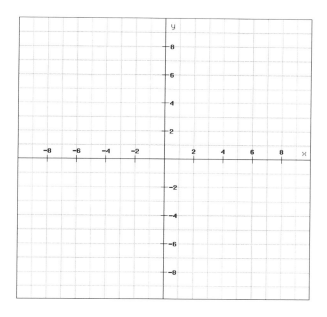

LINES

2. Indicate the following points on the plane: A(0,0), B(1, 1), C(–2, –2), D(6,6)

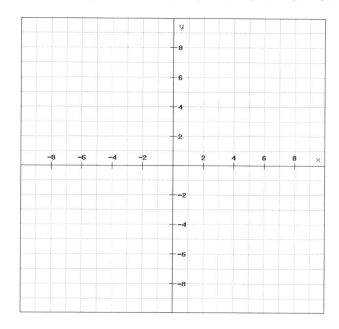

   a. What do these points have in common?

   b. Could you describe all the points that satisfy this property? How?

3. Indicate the following points on the plane: A(0,0), B(1, 2), C(–2, –4), D(4,8)

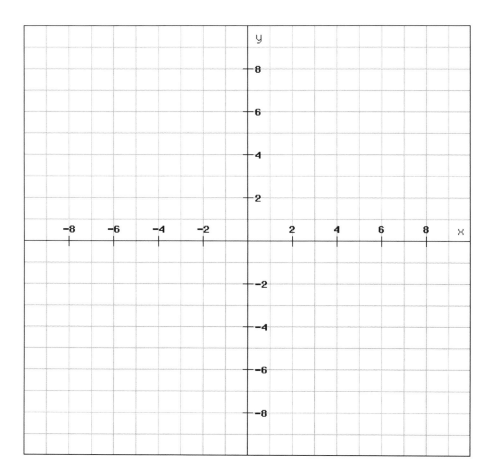

    a. What do these points have in common? Use a ruler to draw the line that connects them.

    b. Could you describe all the points that satisfy this property? How?

    c. On the same graph sketch the following points E(0,1), F(1, 3), G(–2, –3), H(4,9)

    d. What do these points have in common? Use a ruler to draw the line that connects them. What is the relation between this line and the previous line?

4. Indicate the following points on the plane: A(0, –2), B(1, 1), C(2, 4), D(–2,–8)

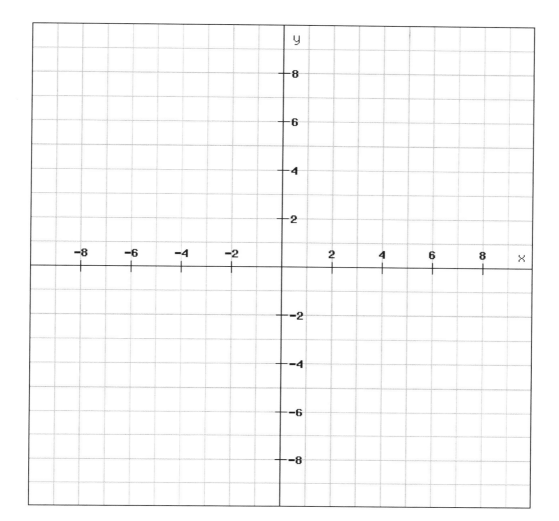

a. What do these points have in common? Use a ruler to draw the line that connects them.

b. Could you describe all the points that satisfy this property? How?

c. On the same graph sketch the following points E(0,1), F(1, 4), G(–2, –5), H(2, 7)

d. What do these points have in common? Use a ruler to draw the line that connects them. What is the relation between this line and the previous line?

2.2. – ANGLES

1. An angle is the figure formed by _____ lines called _____ that start at a common point.

   For example:

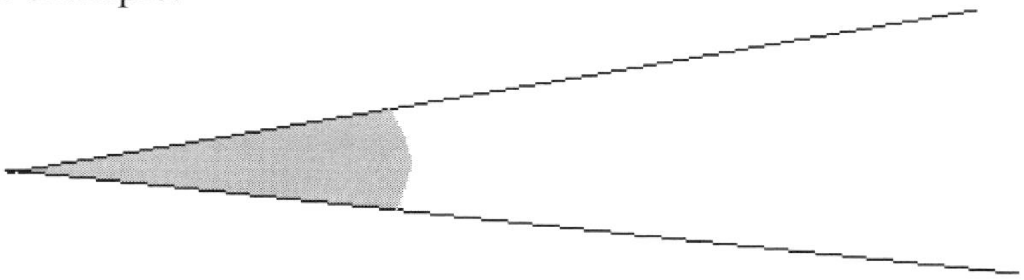

2. A straight angle is: _____

3. An acute angle is: _____

4. A right angle is: _____

5. An obtuse angle is: _____

6. Given the following diagram:

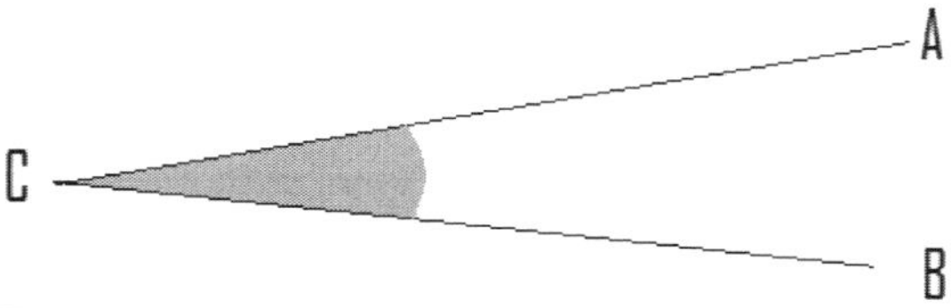

   a. CA and CB are _____

   b. The shaded angle can be called _____ or _____

7. We say that the following angle has a size of _____ degrees or ____ °

8. Use the following square to sketch an angle of 45° degrees:

9. Two angles are complementary if their sum is _____

10. Two angles are supplementary if their sum is _____

11. The complementary of 20° is _____. The complementary of x° is _____

12. The supplementary of 20° is _____. The supplementary of x° is _____

13. The complementary of 42° is _____. The complementary of x° is _____

14. The supplementary of 126° is _____. The supplementary of x° is _____

15. The complementary of 81° is _____. The complementary of x° is _____

16. The supplementary of 0° is _____. The supplementary of x° is _____

17. Find all the unknown angles:

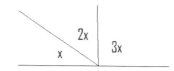

18. Find all the unknown angles:

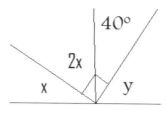

19. Straight lines are _____ or _____

20. Given the following diagram:

   a. The angles x and y are _____

   b. The angles x and a are _____

   c. The angles y and b are _____

21. Given the following diagram:

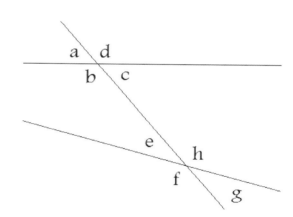

   a. The angles a and e are _____

   b. The angles b and e are _____

   c. The angles b and f are _____

   d. The angles c and e are _____

   e. The angles h and b are _____

   f. The angles e and g are _____

   g. The angles c and h are _____

   h. The angles g and h are _____

   i. The angles b and d are _____

   j. Which angle is a corresponding angle pair with g? _____

   k. Which angle is an alternate angle pair with g? _____

   l. Which angle is a co-interior angle pair with e? _____

Given the following diagram in which the transversal intersects 2 parallel lines:

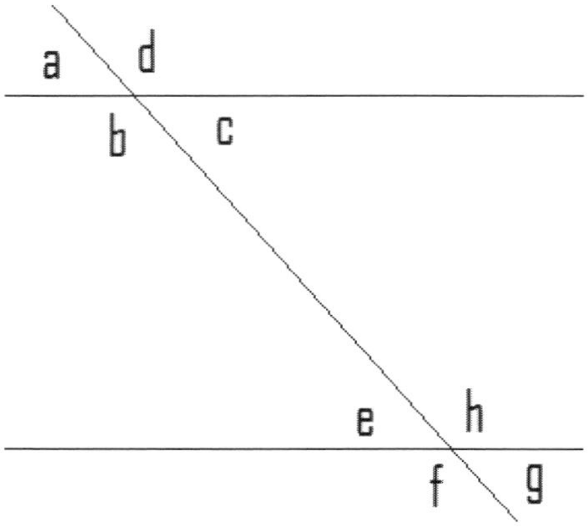

m. The angles a and e are _____

n. The angles b and e are _____

o. The angles b and f are _____

p. The angles c and e are _____

q. The angles h and b are _____

r. The angles e and g are _____

s. The angles c and h are _____

22. Determine if the lines are parallel, explain why: Find all possible angles

$100°$

$79°$

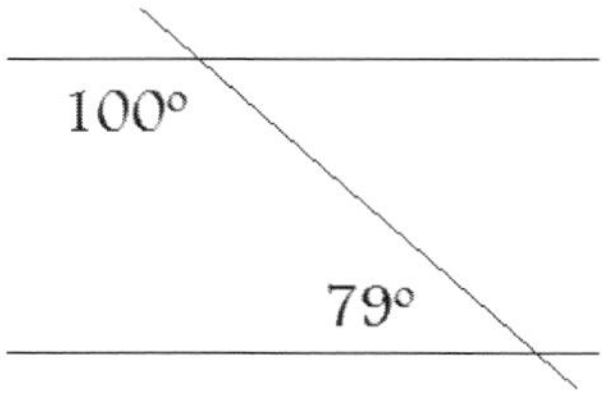

23. Determine if the lines are parallel, explain why: Find all possible angles

$100°$

$100°$

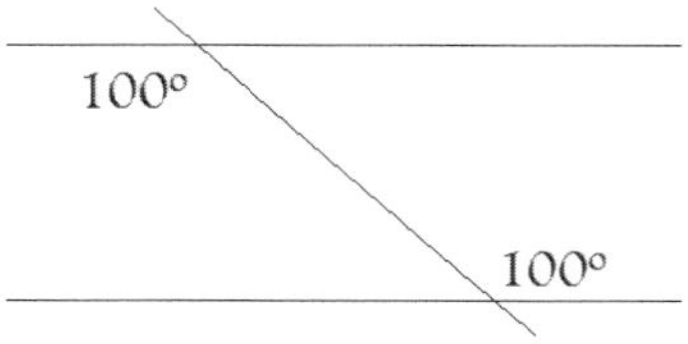

24. Determine if the lines are parallel, explain why Find all possible angles

$50°$

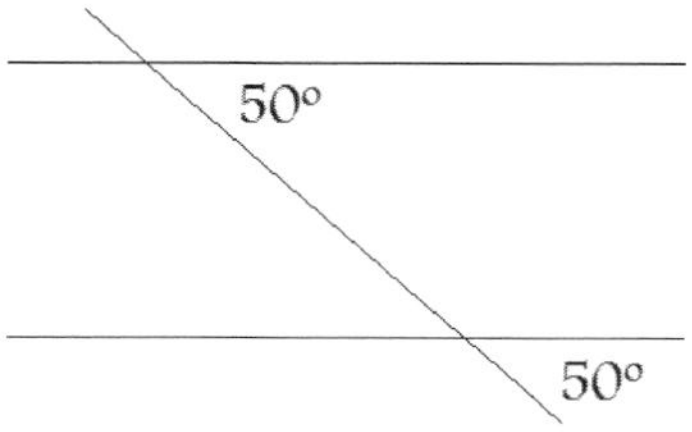

25. Sketch corresponding angle:

$50°$

26. Sketch alternate interior angles:

136

27. Sketch alternate exterior angles:

     _____

     _____

28. Given the AB is parallel to CD, find the angles a, b, c, d, e.

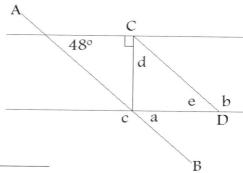

29. The sum of the angles in a triangle is _____

30. The sum of the angles in a square is _____

31. The sum of the angles in a rectangle is _____

32. The sum of the angles in a quadrilateral is _____

33. The sum of the angles in a pentagon is _____

34. The sum of the angles in an hexagon is _____

35. The sum of the angles in an heptagon is _____

36. The sum of the angles in an octagon is _____

37. The sum of the angles in a shape with n sides is _____,

    the reason is that _____

38. Find the regular polygons with which you can fill the floor with tiles. Explain why does this happen.

2.3. – SQUARES, RECTANGLES AND TRIANGLES

1. Indicate the following points on the plane: A(0, 6), B(6, 0), C(0, 0)

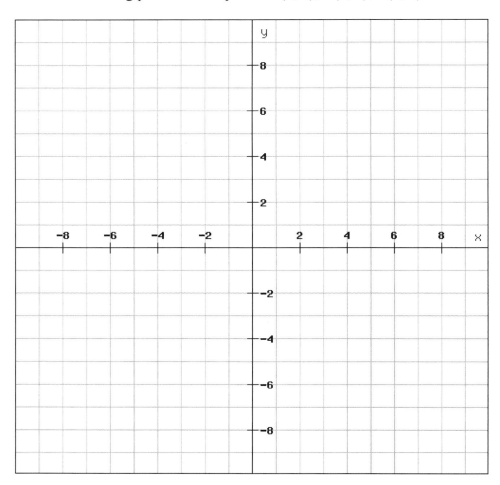

   a. Use a ruler to draw the line that connects each pair of points to form a triangle.

   b. Find all the angles of the triangles you can.

   c. This kind of triangle is called _____ and _____

   d. Write down the lengths of the 2 equal sides: _____

   e. Write down the Pythagorean Theorem: _____.

     This theorem is only true in _____ triangles.

   f. Use P. Theorem to find the length of the third side of the triangle.

   g. Add the point D(6, 6) to the graph. The form ABCD is a _____. The

     area of this shape is _____

   h. Use the area of the square to find the area of the triangle.

2. Indicate the following points on the plane: A(–4, 0), B(2, 6), C(8, 0)

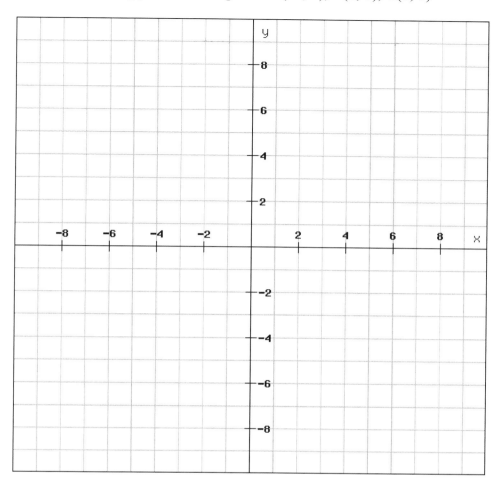

a. Use a ruler to draw the line that connects each pair of points to form a triangle.

b. This kind of triangle is called _____

c. Write down the Pythagorean Theorem: _____.

   This theorem is only true in _____ triangles.

d. Add the point D (2, 0) to the graph. The triangle ABD is _____.

e. The length of AD is _____. The Length of BD is _____. Use P. Theorem to

   find the length of AB.

f. In consequence state the length of BC:_____.

g. The perimeter of the triangle ABC is _____

h. Add the point E (–4, 6) to the graph. The shape AEBD is a _____. The area

   of this shape is ____. Use this area to find the area of the triangle ABD and ABC.

3. Indicate the following points on the plane: A(–6, 0), B(3, 6), C(5, 0)

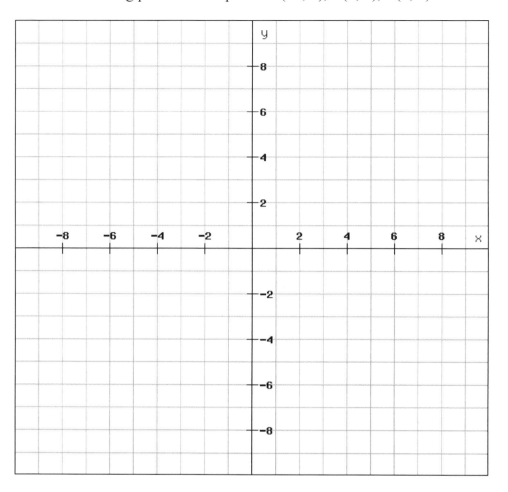

a. Use a ruler to draw the line that connects each pair of points to form a triangle.

b. Is this triangle isosceles or right angled?

c. Add the points D (–6, 6) and E (5, 6) to the graph. The shape ADEC is a _____

    The area of this shape is _____.

d. Add the point F (3, 0) to graph and use the corresponding theorem to find the

    length of AB: _____ and BC _____.

e. The perimeter of the triangle ABC is _____

f. The line BF is called the _____ of the triangle.

g. Every triangle has ____ heights. A height is a lines that starts at a _____

    and ends at _____ forming an angle of _____ with it.

h. Find the area of the triangles ABF, FBC and ABC.

4. Indicate the following points on the plane: A (–5, 0), B (5, 0), C (0, $\sqrt{75}$)

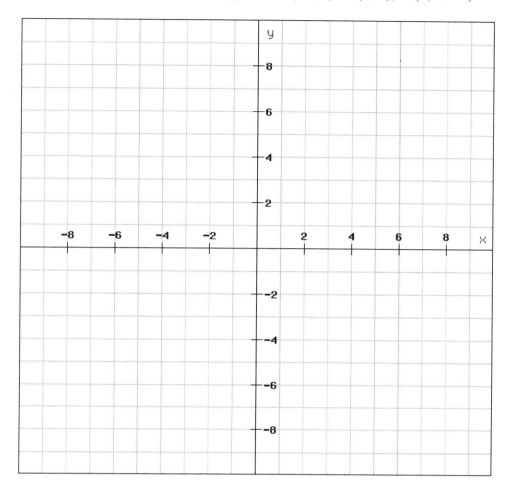

a. Use a ruler to draw the line that connects each pair of points to form a triangle.

b. Add the points D (0, 0) to the graph and use the corresponding theorem to find

length of AB: _____ and BC _____.

c. What kind of triangle is this? _____

d. What can you say about the angles of this triangle?

e. The perimeter of the triangle ABC is _____

f. Find the area of the triangle ABC.

5. Define and sketch an example, include all the known angles and lengths of sides in your example.

    a. Equilateral triangle: c. Right angled triangle:

    b. Isosceles triangle: d. Right angled and isosceles triangle:

6. The vertex angle of an isosceles triangle is 42°, find the size of its base angle.

7. The vertex angle of an isosceles triangle is 110°, find the size of its base angle.

8. The base angle of an isosceles triangle is 50°, find the size of its vertex angle.

9. The base angle of an isosceles triangle is 33°, find the size of its vertex angle.

10. Given the isosceles triangle:

    y = ___ a = ___ b = ___

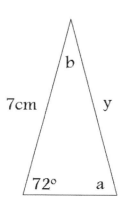

11. Given the diagram, find:

   x = ___ y = ___ a = ___ b = ___

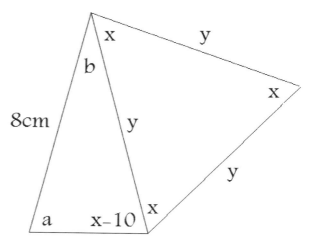

12. The base of an isosceles triangle is 10 cm, its side is 12 cm. Find its perimeter and area.

13. The base angle of an isosceles triangle is 5x + 7, the vertex angle is 2x – 2; find the size of the angles.

14. The base angle of an isosceles triangle is 9x – 10, the vertex angle is 12x – 10; find the size of the angles.

15. Given the following triangle, it is known that AB = 10cm, AD = 7cm and DC = 4cm. Angle CDB = 90°. Find:

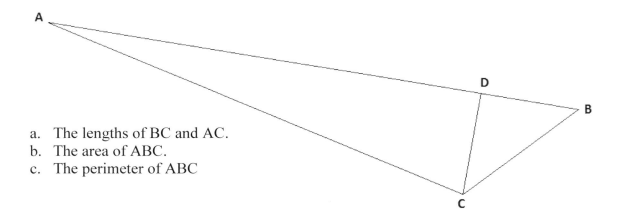

a. The lengths of BC and AC.
b. The area of ABC.
c. The perimeter of ABC

16. Given the following triangle, it is known that AC = 13cm, DB = 4cm and DC = 5cm. Angle CDB = 90°. Find:

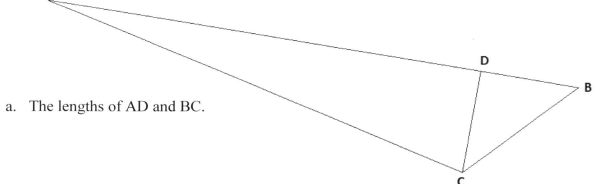

a. The lengths of AD and BC.

b. The area of DCB.

c. The perimeter of ABC

17. Given the following triangle, it is known that AC = 20cm, DB = 10cm and DC = 11 cm. Angle CDB = 90° and angle CEA = 90°. Find:

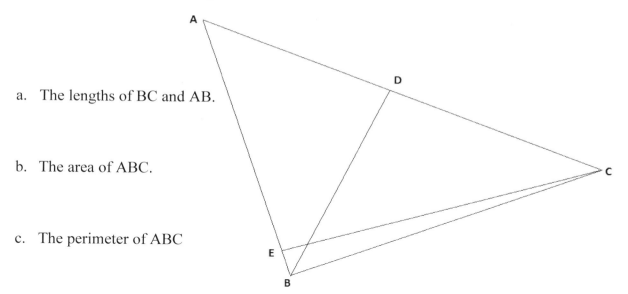

a. The lengths of BC and AB.

b. The area of ABC.

c. The perimeter of ABC

d. What do EC and BD have in common?

e. The lengths of EC, EB and AE

18. Find the perimeter and area of an isosceles right angled triangle whose <u>leg</u> is 10cm.

19. Find the perimeter and area of a right angled triangle whose sides are $6, x, 10$

20. Find the perimeter and area of a right angled triangle whose sides are $\sqrt{x}, \sqrt{x}, \dfrac{x}{2}$

21. Find the area of an isosceles right angled triangle whose <u>perimeter</u> is 20cm.

22. Find the area of an equilateral triangle whose perimeter is 30cm.

23. Given a right angled isosceles triangle whose longest side is 10 cm long.

    a. Sketch the triangle.
    b. Find the perimeter of the triangle.
    c. Find the area of the triangle.

24. Given a right angled isosceles triangle whose smallest side is X cm long.

    a.   Sketch the triangle.
    b.   Find the perimeter of the triangle in terms of X.
    c.   Find the area of the triangle in terms of X.

25. Given an equilateral triangle whose side is 10 cm long.

    a.   Sketch the triangle.
    b.   Find the perimeter of the triangle.
    c.   Find the area of the triangle.

26. Given an equilateral triangle whose side is X cm long.

    a. Sketch the triangle.
    b. Find the perimeter of the triangle in terms of X.
    c. Find the area of the triangle in terms of X.

27. Find the perimeter of an isosceles triangle whose base is half of its side and its area is 20 cm^2

28. Find the perimeter of an isosceles triangle whose base is a third of its side and its area is A cm^2, in terms of A.

29. Find the area of a right angled triangle in which 1 leg is 10% <u>longer</u> than the other and whose perimeter is 70cm

30. Find the area of a right angled triangle in which 1 leg is 25% <u>shorter</u> than the other and whose perimeter is 24cm

31. Given the following diagram (not to scale), BD = x cm, DC = 3BD, AD = 10 cm, AC = 20cm

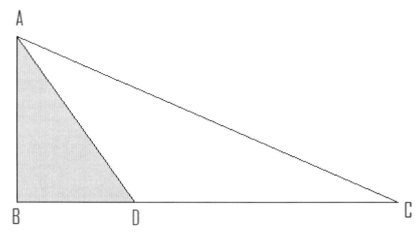

a. Write 2 equations with the given information.

b. Solve the equations to determine x.

c. Find the perimeter and area of ABC.

d. Find the perimeter and area of ABD.

e. Find the perimeter and area of ADC.

f. Determine the percentage of the area that is shaded.

30. Given the following diagram (not to scale), BD = 8 cm, AD = 17 , DC = 104 cm,

a. Find the perimeter and area of ABC

b. Find the perimeter and area of ABD.

c. Find the perimeter and area of ADC.

d. Determine the percentage of the area that is shaded.

e. Determine the percentage by which the area of ABC is bigger than ABD

f. Determine the percentage by which the area of ABC is bigger than ADC

g. Determine the percentage by which the area of ADC is bigger than ABD

h. Determine the percentage by which the area of ABD is smaller than ABC

i. Determine the percentage by which the area of ADC is smaller than ABC

j. Determine the percentage by which the area of ABD is smaller than ADC

k. Determine the percentage by which the perimeter of ABC is bigger than ABD

l. Determine the percentage by which the perimeter of ABC is bigger than ADC

m. Determine the percentage by which the perimeter of ADC is bigger than ABD

n. Determine the percentage by which the perimeter of ABD is smaller than ABC

o. Determine the percentage by which the perimeter of ADC is smaller than ABC

p. Determine the percentage by which the perimeter of ABD is smaller than ADC

2.4. – POINTS OF CONCURRENCY

1. Given the following triangle, sketch all the <u>altitudes</u> in the triangle.

   An altitude is: _____. The point where

   they meet is called "<u>orthocenter</u>". Name the point H.

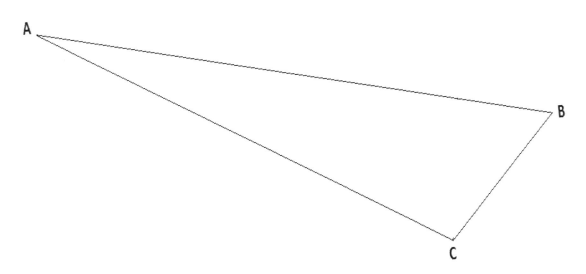

2. Given the following triangle, Sketch all the <u>perpendicular bisectors</u> in the triangle.

   The point where they meet is called <u>circumcenter</u>, it is the centre of _____

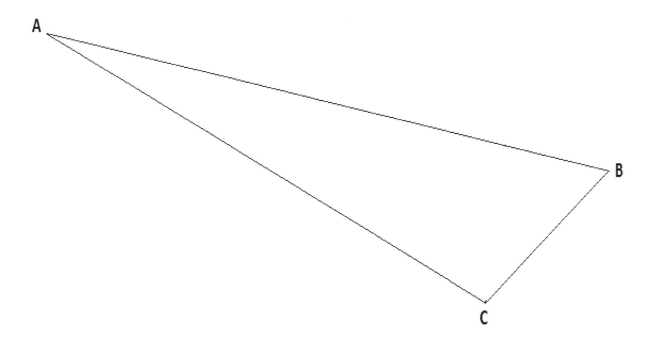

3. Given the following triangle, Sketch all the <u>angle bisectors</u> in the triangle.

   The point where they meet is called incenter, it is the centre of _____

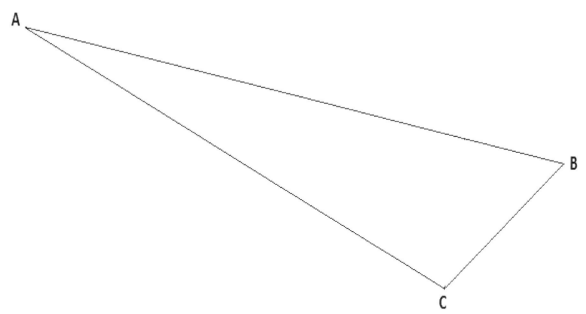

4. Given the following triangle, Sketch all the medians in the triangle.

   The point where they meet is called centroid. If the centroid is M then the following

   relations are satisfied (complete):

   $$AM = \frac{2}{3} AD \qquad\qquad BM = \qquad\qquad CM =$$

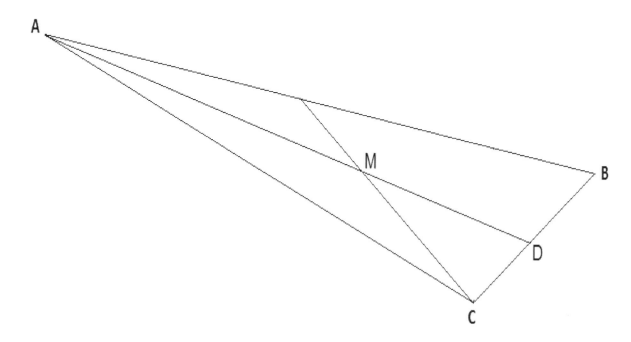

5. The Incentre is: _____

6. The Orthocentre is: _____

7. The Circumcentre is: _____

8. The Centroid is: _____

9. The Circumcentre is equidistant to _____

10. The Incentre is equidistant to _____

11. Given that the coordinates of a triangle are A(-6, 0). B(4, 0), C(2, 8)

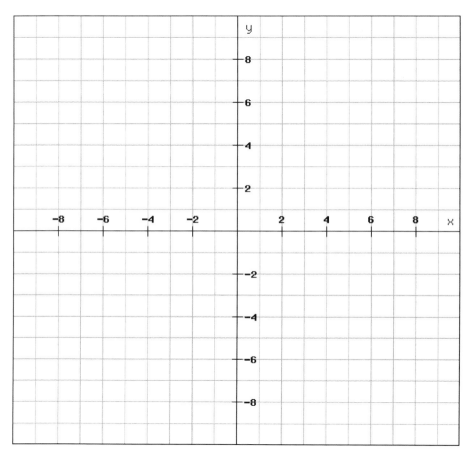

    a. Sketch the triangle.
    b. Graphically find its orthocentre.
    c. Calculate the coordinates of its orthocentre.

12. Given that the coordinates of a triangle are A(-6, 0). B(4, 0), C(2, 8)

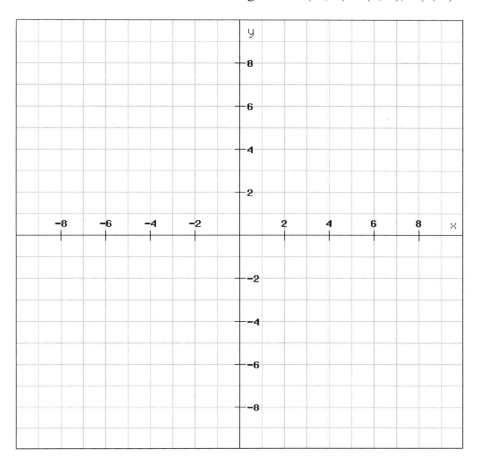

a. Sketch the triangle.
b. Graphically find its circumcenter.
c. Find the points D. E, F the bisectors of AB, BC, and AC correspondingly.
d. Find the slope of the lines AB, BC, find the perpendicular slopes.
e. Use the previous part to construct 2 of the perpendicular bisectors and find their point of intersection which is the circumcenter

13. Given that the coordinates of a triangle are A(-6, 2). B(4, 8), C(0, -8)

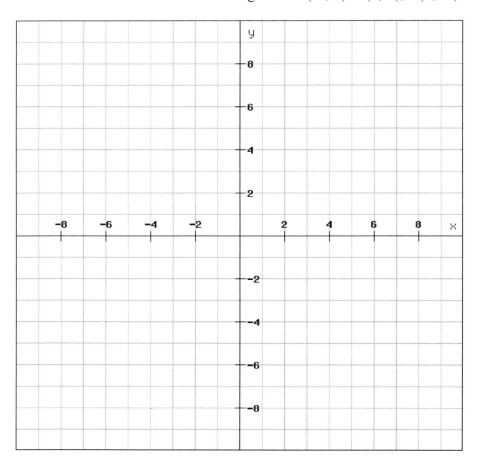

    a. Sketch the triangle.
    b. Graphically find its incentre.
    c. Find the coordinates of the incentre.

14. Given that the coordinates of a triangle are A(-6, 2). B(4, 8), C(0, -8)

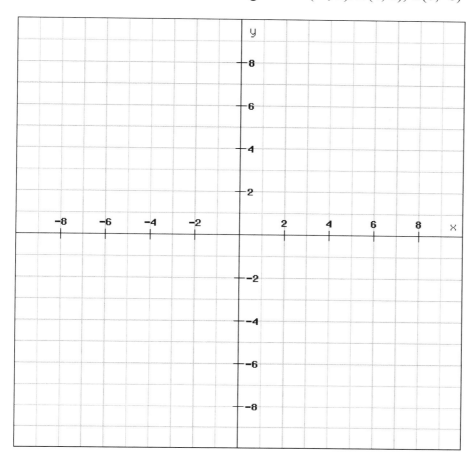

   a. Sketch the triangle.
   b. Graphically find its centroid.
   c. Calculate the coordinates of its centroid.

2.5. – CONGRUENT AND SIMILAR TRIANGLES

1. 2 triangles are similar if all of their angles are _____

2. 2 triangles are similar if <u>any</u> of the following is satisfied:

    a. 2 of their angles are _____. Sketch an example:

    b. 2 of their sides are _____ and the angles between them are _____. Sketch an example:

    c. All their sides are _____. Sketch an example:

3. All right angled triangles are similar True / False. Sketch an example to show answer:

4. Congruent triangles are similar triangles with ratio of proportionality _____

5. Similar triangles are always congruent True/False

6. congruent triangles are always Similar True/False

7. Determine if the following pair of triangles are similar, give a reason:

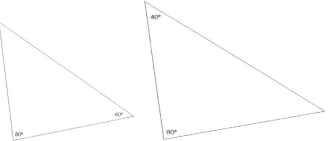

8. Determine if the following pair of triangles are similar, give a reason:

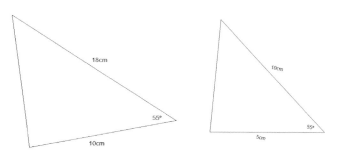

9. Determine if the following pair of triangles are similar, give a reason:

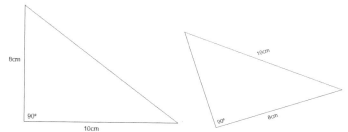

10. Determine if the following pair of triangles are similar, give a reason:

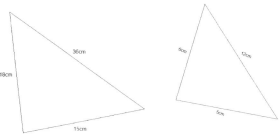

11. Determine if the following pair of triangles are similar, give a reason:

12. Determine if the following pair of triangles are similar, give a reason:

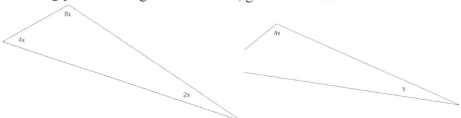

13. Given that $AB \parallel CD$, determine if the triangles ABE and CED are similar, give a reason:

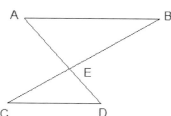

14. Given that $BC \parallel DE$, determine if the triangles ABC and ADE are similar, give a reason:

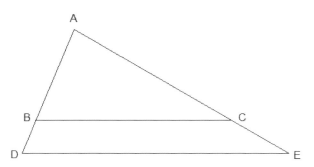

15. The shadow of a man formed by a street light on the ground is equal to twice its height. If the man is 10m away from the street light and his height is 1.80m, how high is the street light?

16. Given that $AB \parallel CD$, find ED:

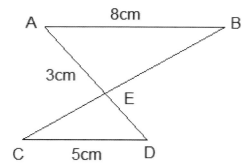

17. In the following triangle the angle BAC is a right angle. AD is an altitude from A to the BC. Show that triangles ABC, ADB and ADC are all similar. If BC = 10cm and AD = 2DC find the perimeter and area of ABD.

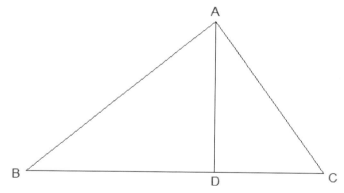

18. The following triangle AB = AC. AD is a altitude from A to the BC. Show that triangles ABD and ACD are similar. If BD = x and 2AB = 3AD, find the perimeter and area of ABC in terms of x.

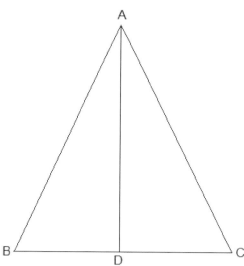

19. To measure the height of building the following operation can be performed. Jeff whose height is 180 cm puts a mirror at a distance of 22 m from a building and observed the top of the building in the mirror standing 0.4 m from it. Find the height of the building.

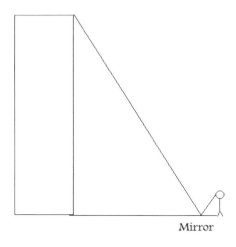

Mirror

20. Given the facade of a certain house, it is known that AC = 4m, CD = 2AC, CE = 7m DE = 3m. ABCD is a rectangle.
Find:

a. The height of the house above ground (help: lower a altitude from E).

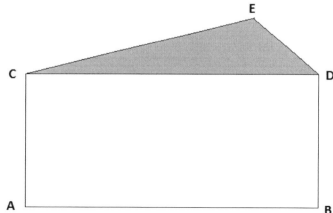

b. The area of the entire facade.

2.6. – DISTANCE AND MIDPOINT

1. Indicate the following points on the plane: A(2,3), B(6, 9), C(−3, −7), D(6,−5)

   a. Add the point (6, 3) and use Pythagorean Theorem to find the distance between the points A and B.

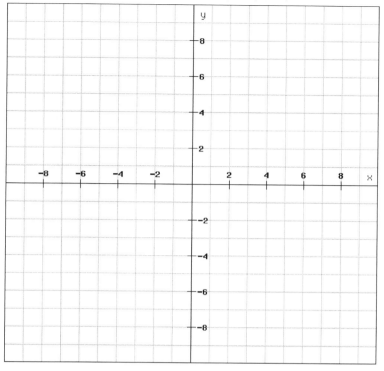

   b. Add the point (−3,−5) and use Pythagorean Theorem to find the distance between the points C and D.

   c. Find the distance AC

   d. Find the midpoint between AB (help: the midpoint x coordinate is the "average" of the x coordinates and the y coordinate is the "average" of the y coordinates)

   e. Find the midpoint between CD

   f. Find the midpoint between AC

2. Find the distance between (1, 3) and (7, −3), find the mid point.

3. Find the distance between (a, b) and (c, d), find the mid point.

4. Find a point whose distance to the point (2, 1) is 7.

5. Find a point whose distance to the point (–4, 2) is 3, can you draw a conclusion about such points in general?

6. The midpoint between the points (*a*, 5) and (–2, b) is (0, 0) find *a* and b.

7. The midpoint between the points (1+x, 2) and (–2+3x, 2 – y) is (1, 1) find x and y.

8. Given that the mid point between A(2, 5) and B is M(3, –2). Find point B.

9. Given that the mid point between A(–6, 4) and B is M(10, 0). Find point B.

10. Given that AB = BC = CD and A, B, C and D are aligned. Point A is (2, 4) and point D is (10, 10). Find points B and C.

11. Given that the distance AB = BC = CD. A, B, C, D are aligned. Point A is (–4, 8) and point B is (–2, 1). Find points C and D.

12. Given points A(3, –2), B(6, 1) and C(0, a). It is known that AC = BC, find a.

13. Given points A(–12, –8), B(–4, 7) and C(a, 0). It is known that AC = BC, find a.

2.7. – CIRCLES

1. Given the following circle:

   a. Sketch a diameter.
   b. Sketch a radius.
   c. The diameter is _____ the radius
   d. Sketch a chord smaller than the diameter
   e. Sketch a chord smaller than the radius

2. Given the following circle:

   a. Sketch a 60° angle.
   b. Show the corresponding minor arc/major arc
   c. Choose 3 points on the circle, connect them with chords. The triangle formed is inscribed in the circle. The circle is circumscribed about the triangle.
   d. Chords that are at the same distance from the centre are _____

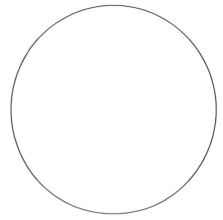

3. Given the following circle:

   a. Choose 3 points on the circle, name them A, B and C. Sketch AB and BC. The angle ABC is inscribed in the circle.
   b. Choose a 4th point on the circle, name it D. Sketch AD and CD. The angle ADC is inscribed in the circle.
   c. What is your conclusion?

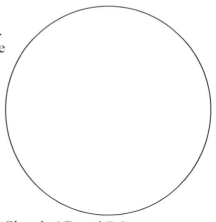

4. Given the following circle:

   a. Choose 3 points on the circle, name them A, B and C. Sketch AB and BC. The angle ABC is inscribed in the circle.
   b. Sketch the center of the circle; name it O. Sketch AO and CO. The angle AOC is inscribed in the circle.
   c. What is your conclusion?

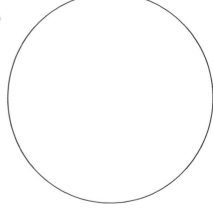

5. Given the following circle:

    a. Sketch the diameter of the circle; name it AC. Sketch a 3rd point B. Connect AB, AC and BC. The angle ABC is inscribed in the circle. Its size is: _____
    b. Choose a 4th point on the circle; name it D. Connect AD, DC. The angle ADC is inscribed in the circle. Its size is: _____

    c. What is your conclusion?

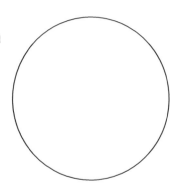

6. Find the missing angles, o is the centre of the circle:

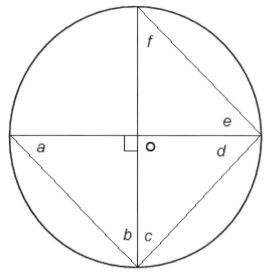

7. Find the missing angles, o is the centre of the circle:

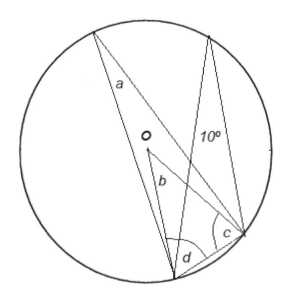

166

8. Find the missing angles, o is the centre of the circle:

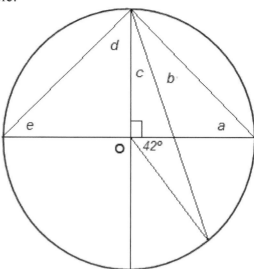

9. Find the missing angles, o is the centre of the circle:

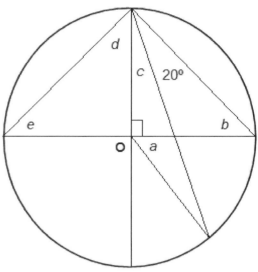

10. Find the missing angles, o is the centre of the circle:

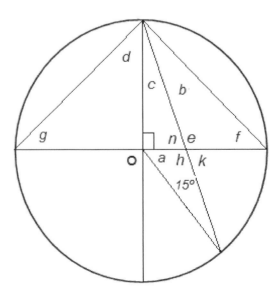

11. Given the following circle:

Sketch the diameter of the circle; name it AC. Sketch a 3rd point B. Connect AB, AC and BC. Given that the radius of the circle is 1cm and AB = 1cm find the perimeter of ABC.

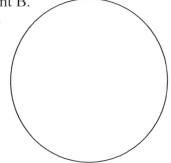

12. Sketch a chord whose length is half of the diameter. In case the radius is 2cm find the area and perimeter of the triangle formed by connecting the center of the circle with the ends of the chord.

13. Given a circle with radius R, find

The Perimeter of the circle: _____

The Area of the circle: _____

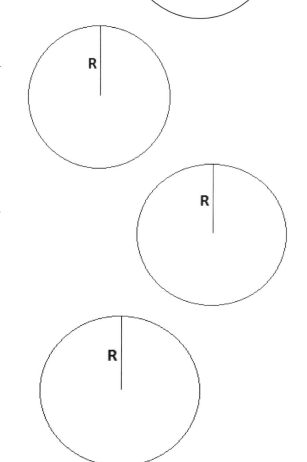

14. Given a circle with radius $\dfrac{4}{\pi}$ cm, find

The Perimeter of the circle: _____

The Area of the circle: _____

15. Given a circle with perimeter 20π cm, find

The radius of the circle: _____

The Area of the circle: _____

16. Given a circle with area 16π cm^2, find

   The radius of the circle: _____

   The perimeter of the circle: _____

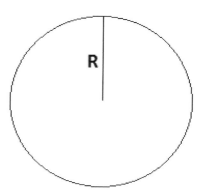

17. Shade 10% of the figure, find the corresponding angle. The length
   Of an arc in a circle is L = _____

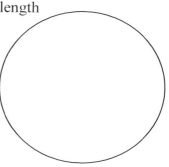

18. Given that R = 5 cm. Shade 20% of the figure, find the corresponding angle and
   the area shaded. Find the perimeter of the shaded area.

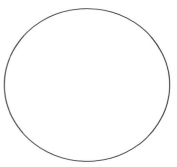

19. Given that R = 15 cm. Shade 30% of the figure, write the corresponding angle
   and find the area shaded. Find the perimeter of the shaded area.

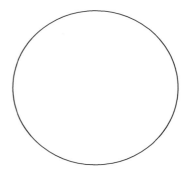

20. Given a circle with radius 10cm:

    a.   Find the <u>percentage</u> of the area shaded.
    b.   Find the <u>size</u> of the shaded area.
    c.   Find the <u>perimeter</u> of the shaded area.

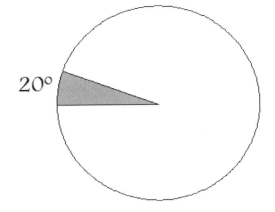

21. Given a circle with radius 10cm:

    a.   Find the <u>percentage</u> of the shaded area of the total area of the circle in terms of the angel x.
    b.   Find the <u>size</u> of the shaded area in terms of x.
    c.   Find the <u>perimeter</u> of the shaded area in terms of x.

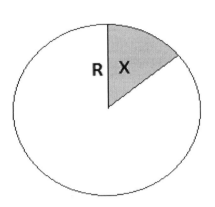

22. The length of the perimeter of a circle with radius r is _____. The length of the arc that corresponds an angle x° is _____. In case the angle x is measured in radians it would be _____.

The area of a circle with radius r is _____. The area of the sector that corresponds an angle x° is _____. In case the angle x is measured in radians it would be _____.

23. Given the circle with r = 2cm :

    a. Show the arc corresponding an angle of 45°.
    b. Calculate its length.
    c. Shade the corresponding sector area.
    d. Calculate it.

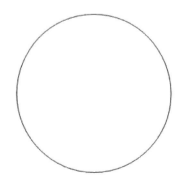

24. Given the circle with r = 3.2m:

    a. Show the arc corresponding an angle of 20°.
    b. Calculate its length.
    c. Shade the corresponding sector area.
    d. Calculate it.

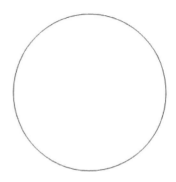

25. Given the circle with r = 3m:
    a. Show the arc corresponding an angle of 18°.
    b. Calculate its length.
    c. Calculate its perimeter.
    d. Shade the corresponding sector area.
    e. Calculate it.

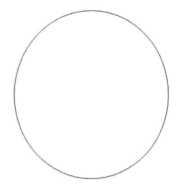

26. Given the circle with r = 6m:

    a. Show the arc corresponding an angle of 50°
    b. Calculate its length.
    c. Shade the corresponding sector area.
    d. Calculate it.

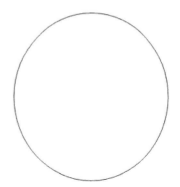

27. Given the following concentric circles with radii 3 cm and 5 cm correspondingly. Find the shaded area.

28. Given the following concentric circles with radii 10m and 14m correspondingly. Calculate the shaded area.

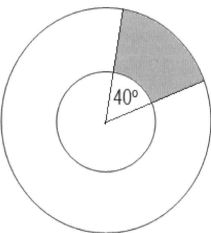

29. Given the following circle, AB is a chord on a circle with radius 10cm Calculate the shaded area.

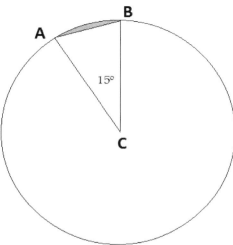

30. Given a circle with radius 8 cm. The segments AB and AC are tangent to the circle. Find the shaded area.

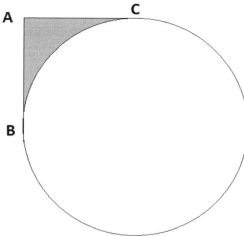

31. Given a circle with radius 10cm in which a square is circumscribed

    a.   Find the length of the side of the square.
    b.   Find the area of the square.
    c.   Find the area of the circle
    d.   Find the percentage of the area of the circle that the square occupies.

32. Given a circle with radius 10cm circumscribed in a square:

    a.   Find the length of the side of the square.
    b.   Find the area of the square.
    c.   Find the area of the circle
    d.   Find the percentage of the area of the square that the circle occupies.

33. On the following diagram sketch the following directions:

    a. N
    b. N30°E
    c. N45°E
    d. E45°N
    e. S10°W
    f. W80°S
    g. W20°N
    h. N30°W

State a conclusion about the "uniqueness" of a direction.

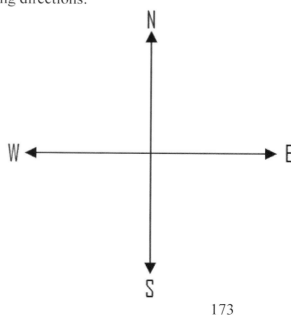

2.8. – QUADRILATERAS

1. Given the following table, fill the blank using *a, b, c, d, h, r*

	Shape	Area	Perimeter
Square			
Rectangle			
Parallelogram			
Isosceles Trapezoid			
Trapezpezoid			
Rhombus			
Kite			

2. Given the following quadrilaterals. Write the name of each one of them:

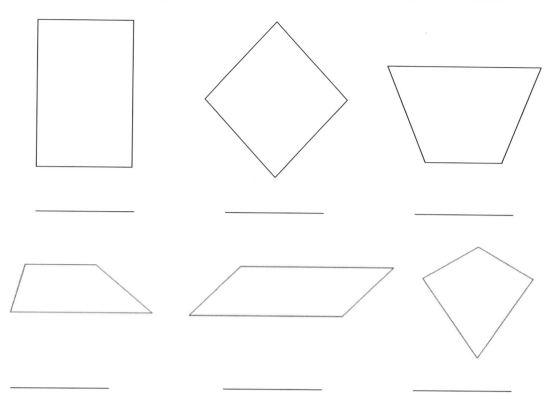

3. Given the following table, fill the blanks with yes or no.

	Shape (sketch)	Only 1 pair of parallel sides	2 pairs of parallel sides	1 pair of equal sides	2 pairs of equal sides	4 equal sides
Square						
Rectangle						
Parallelogram						
Isosceles Trapezoid						
Trapezoid						
Rhombus						
Kite						

4. True or False

    a. A square is also a parallelogram   True / False

    b. A square is also a rectangle   True / False

    c. A square is also a trapezoid   True / False

    d. A parallelogram is also a square   True / False

    e. A rectangle is also a square   True / False

    f. A rhombus is always a parallelogram   True / False

    g. A parallelogram is always r rhombus   True / False

    h. A parallelogram is sometimes a rhombus   True / False

    i. A rhombus is always a kite   True / False

    j. All the shapes above mentioned are quadrilaterals True / False

5. Given the following table, fill the blanks with yes or no.

	Shape (Sketch diagonals as well)	Diagonals are perpendicular	Diagonals are equal	Diagonals bisect angle	Diagonals bisect each other
Square					
Rectangle					
Parallelogram					
Isosceles Trapezoid					
Trapezoid					
Rhombus					
Kite					

6. Given a square with diagonal of 4 cm, find its area and perimeter.

7. Given a square with diagonal of a cm, find its area and perimeter.

8. Given a rectangle with diagonal of 7m and one side is twice as large as the other, find its area and perimeter.

9. Given a rectangle with diagonal of 20m and one side is twice as large as the other, find its area and perimeter.

10. Given the following parallelogram. ABC is isosceles and right angled. AB = 2cm, CD = 5cm (Diagram not to scale). Find:

     a. The area and perimeter of the parallelogram
     b. The area and perimeter of ABC
     c. The area and perimeter of BCD
     d. The area and perimeter of CDE

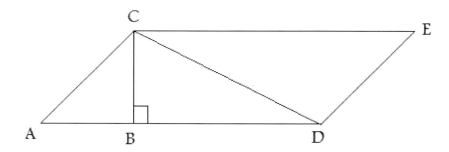

11. Given the following isosceles trapezoid. ABC is right angled. AC = 7cm, CE = 15cm and AE = 20cm (Diagram not to scale). Find:

    a. The area and perimeter of ABC and BCE
    b. The area and perimeter of the trapezoid
    c. The area and perimeter of CDE

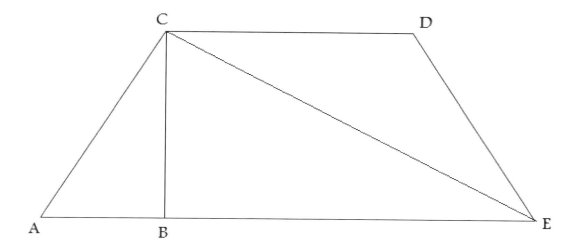

12. Given the following rhombus. BC = 6cm, AD = 18cm and find the area and perimeter the rhombus (Diagram not to scale).

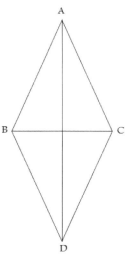

13. Given the following kite. BC = 4cm, AE = 8cm and CD = 2AC find the area and perimeter the kite (Diagram not to scale).

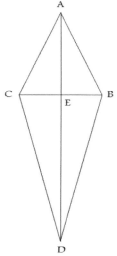

14. It is known that the perimeter of a rhombus with equal diagonals is 40cm. Find its area.

15. Find the side length of a square whose area is equal to its perimeter.

16. Find the side length of a rhombus whose area is equal to its perimeter and one of its diagonals is 5cm long.

2.9. – 3D GEOMETRY

1. Given the following table, fill the blanks

	Shape	Surface Area	Volume
Cuboid (Rectangular Prism)			
Pyramid (Square based)			
Sphere			
Cylinder			
Cone			

2. Given the following table, fill the blanks

	Shape	Surface Area	Volume
Triangular prism			
Triangle based Pyramid (Tetrahedron)			

3. Find the volume and surface area of a sphere with radius 10cm.

4. Find the volume and surface area of a sphere with radius 0.4m.

5. Find the volume of a square based pyramid with base length $2x$ cm and height is x cm.

6. Find the volume and surface area of a square based cuboid whose base length is 15 cm and height 0.1m

7. Find the volume and surface area of a cone with radius 0.4m and height 2m.

8. Find the volume and surface area of a cylinder with radius 0.4m and height 2m.

9. Given that the volume of a square based pyramid is 10 m^3 and that its height is equal to its base length, find the perimeter of its base.

10. Given that the volume of a cuboid is 10 m^3 and that the ratio between its sides is 1:2:3. Find its surface area.

11. Given that the volume of a cone is 10 m^3 and that its height is 3 times the radius of the base. Find its height.

12. Given that the volume of a sphere is 10 m^3. Find its surface area.

13. Find the volume and surface area of the following shape:

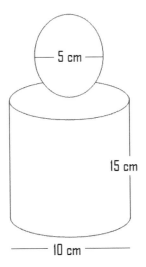

14. Find the volume and surface area of the following shape:

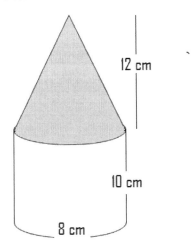

15. Find the volume and surface area of the following shape:

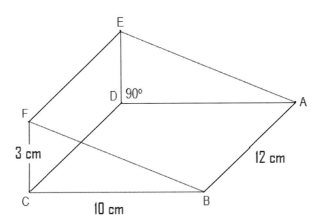

2.10. – GEOMETRIC TRANSOFRMATIONS

1. Indicate the following points on the plane: A(0,0), B(–1,6),C(4,2). Connect them to form a triangle.

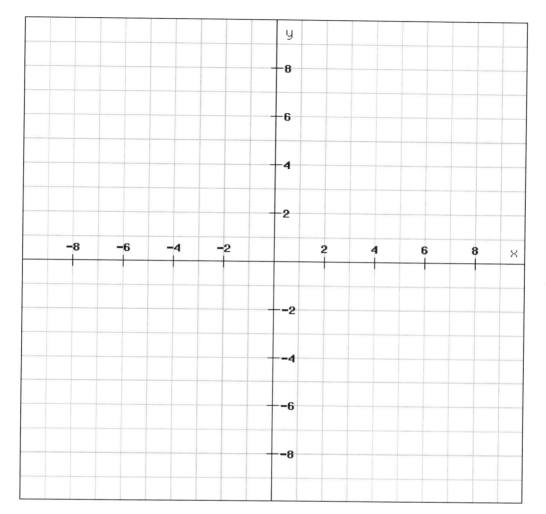

a. Indicate the following points on the plane: A'(0,–3), B'(–1,3),C'(4,–1), Connect them to form a triangle.

b. What can you say about the location of the 2nd triangle in comparison to the first one?

c. This is a _____ translation.

2. Indicate the following points on the plane: A(0,0), B(−1,6),C(4,2). Connect them to form a triangle.

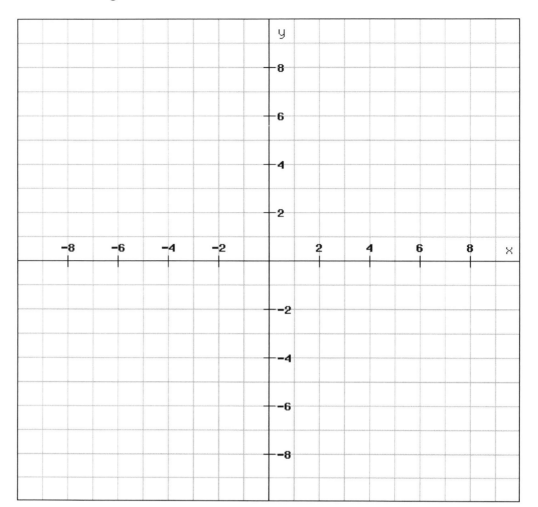

a. Indicate the following points on the plane: A'(4,0), B'(3,6),C'(8,2), Connect them to form a triangle.

b. What can you say about the location of the 2nd triangle in comparison to the first one?

c. This is a _____ translation.

3. Indicate the following points on the plane: A(0,0), B(–1,6),C(4,2). Connect them to form a triangle.

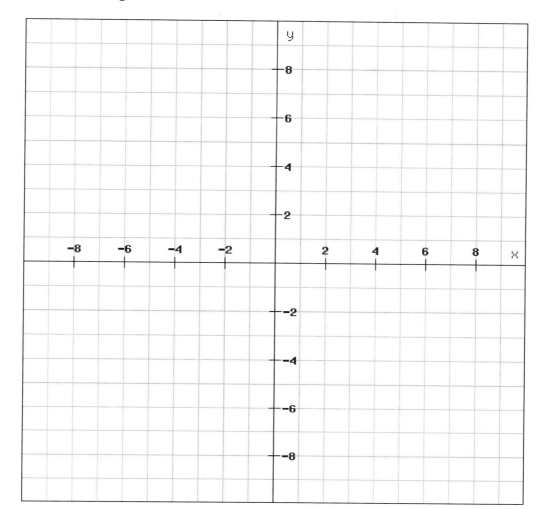

a. Indicate the following points on the plane: A'(–2,–3), B'(–3,3),C'(2,–1), Connect them to form a triangle.

b. What can you say about the location of the 2nd triangle in comparison to the first one?

c. This is a _____ and _____ translations.

4. Indicate the following points on the plane: A(1,0), B(–2,6),C(6,3). Connect them to form a triangle.

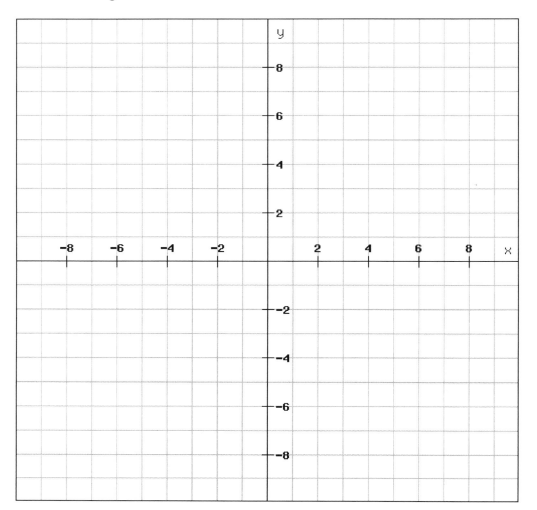

a. Indicate the following points on the plane: A'(–1,0), B'(2,6),C'(–6,3), Connect them to form a triangle.

b. What can you say about the location of the 2nd triangle in comparison to the first one?

c. This is a _____ across the y axis.

d. On changing x into _____ we are generating a _____ across the _____

5. Indicate the following points on the plane: A(1,1), B(–2,6),C(6,3). Connect them to form a triangle.

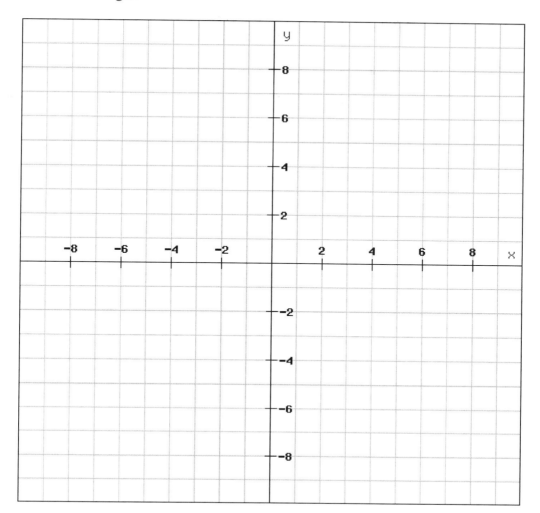

a. Indicate the following points on the plane: A'(1,–1), B'(–2,–6),C'(6,–3), Connect them to form a triangle.

b. What can you say about the location of the 2nd triangle in comparison to the first one?

c. This is a _____ across the x axis.

d. On changing y into _____ we are generating a _____ across the _____

6. Indicate the following points on the plane: A(–4,0), B(0,4),C(4,0), D(0, –4).
   Connect them to form a square.

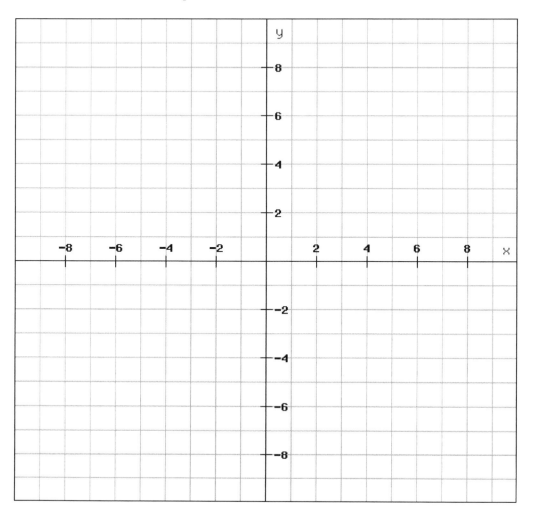

a. Indicate the following points on the plane: $\sqrt{8} \approx 2.83$

   A'$(-\sqrt{8},\sqrt{8})$,B'$(\sqrt{8},\sqrt{8})$, C'$(\sqrt{8},-\sqrt{8})$, D'$(-\sqrt{8},-\sqrt{8})$ Connect them to form a square.

b. What can you say about the location of the 2nd square in comparison to the first one?

c. This is a _____ of _____ degrees.

d. Write down the coordinates of a square that is a rotation of 90° of the first one:

   A'' = (__, __), B'' = (__, __), C'' = (__, __), D'' = (__, __)

   Conclusions?

7. Indicate the following points on the plane: A(–5,0), B(5,0). Given also the point C(0,*a*)

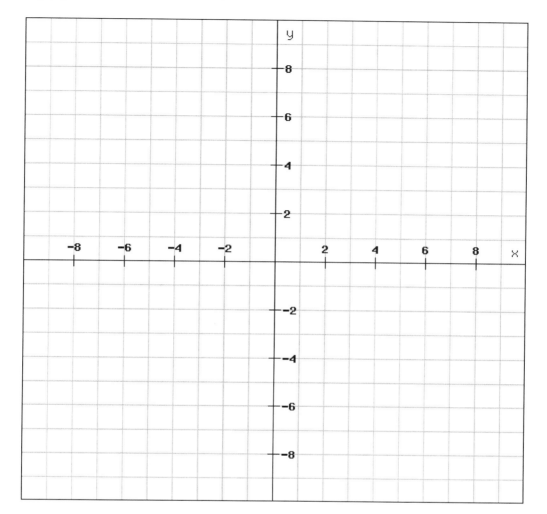

a. Show that the value of *a* in order to create an equilateral triangle is: $\sqrt{75}$
b. Write down the coordinates of the new points after translating the triangle 3 units left and 1 down.

A' = (__,__), B' = (__,__), C' = (__,__)

c. Write down the coordinates of the new points after rotation the triangle 30° clockwise.

A'' = (__,__), B'' = (__,__), C'' = (__,__)

d. Write down the coordinates of the new points after rotation the triangle 60° clockwise.

A''' = (__,__), B''' = (__,__), C''' = (__,__)

8. Indicate the following points on the plane: A(1,0), B(–2,5),C(4,3). Connect them to form a triangle.

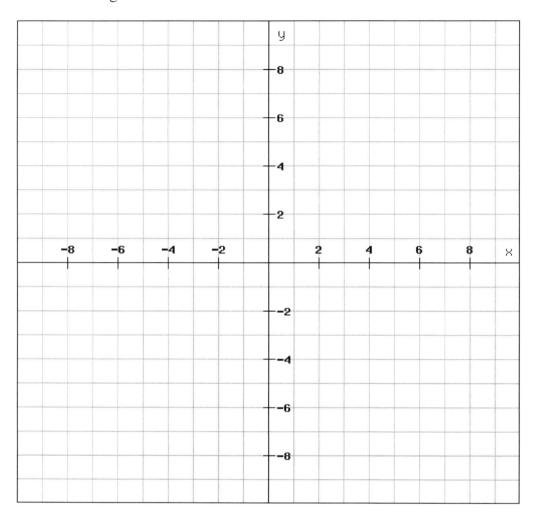

a. Indicate the following points on the plane: A'(2,0), B'(–4,10),C'(8,6), Connect them to form a triangle.

b. What can you say about the 2nd triangle in comparison to the first one?

c. This is a _____ factor _____

d. Indicate the following points on the plane: A'(0.5,0), B'(–1,2.5),C'(2,1.5), Connect them to form a triangle.

e. What can you say about the 2nd triangle in comparison to the first one?

f. This is a _____ factor _____

g. When making all sides of a shape bigger or smaller using the same factor the

shape remains _____ to the original one.

9. Indicate the following points on the plane: A(0,0), B(2, 0),C(0,–3). Connect them to form a triangle.

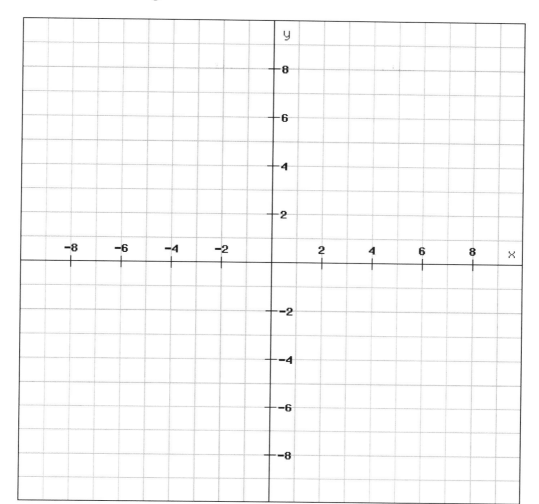

   a. Indicate the points of he triangle formed if we enlarge this triangle by 3.

       A' = (__, __), B' = (__, __), C' = (__, __)

   b. Find the relations:

$$\frac{A'B'}{AB} = \qquad \frac{A'C'}{AC} = \qquad \frac{B'C'}{BC} =$$

10. Given a triangle ABC whose sides are 3, 4 and 5 cm long.

    a. Is his a right angled triangle?

    b. Find the sides of another triangle whose sides are half the length of the sides of ABC. Is this triangle right angled?

11. Given a triangle ABC whose sides are 2, 4 and x cm long. A similar triangle has sides y, 6 and z correspondingly.

    a. Find y

    b. Find $\dfrac{z}{x}$

    c. Is it possible to find a value for x so that ABC will be right angled? If yes, find it (all possibilities).

    d. Find z in that case(s)

12. Given a rectangle ABCD whose sides are 5, and x cm long. A similar rectangle has sides y and 12 cm correspondingly. The perimeter of the 1st rectangle is 8 units longer than the perimeter of the 2nd one.

    a. Find x and y

    b. Find the area of the rectangles A$_1$ and A$_2$.

    c. Find the quotient $\dfrac{A_2}{A_1}$, conclusions?

13. Given that the area of a square is 16 times as big as the area of a different square. Find the ratio between the sides of the squares.

14. Explain the meaning of the operation "Zooming in/out" frequently used in digital imaging.

CHAPTER 3 – FUNCTIONS

3.1. – INTRODUCTION TO FUNCTIONS

1. Try to sketch an approximate graph for the height of a human, add some reasonable numbers to the graph:

Height (cm)

Age (years)

    a. Height(0) = _____, it is the Height of _____

    b. Height(t) = 100cm, t = _____

    c. Write the set of possible values for the Age: _____, this is the Domain

    d. Write the set of possible values for the Height: _____, this is the Range:

    e. This graph describes a function that shows how _____ depends on _____

2. Write the definition of a function in your own words:

3. Write 2 examples of relations that are functions:

4. The independent variable is usually represented in the _____

5. The dependent variable is usually represented in the _____

6. Draw a sketch of 2 functions. Can you write the mathematical expression to describe them?

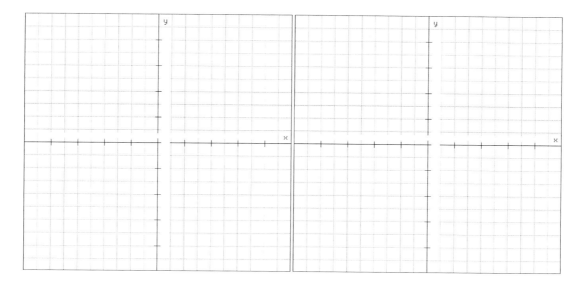

7. Write 2 examples of relations that <u>are not</u> functions:

8. Which one of the following graphs cannot represent function? Explain.

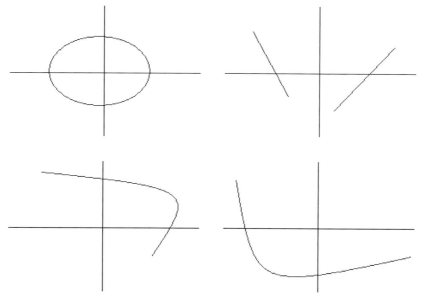

9. Draw an example of a curve that does not represent a function:

10. Draw an example of a curve that represents a function:

11. The domain of a function is the: _____

12. The Range of a function is the: _____

13. Out of the following relations circle the ones that are functions:

    a. Person's name $\rightarrow$ Person's age
    b. City $\rightarrow$ Number of habitants
    c. City $\rightarrow$ Names of habitants
    d. Family $\rightarrow$ Home Address
    e. Satellite's name $\rightarrow$ Position of satellite
    f. Time $\rightarrow$ Position of object
    g. One $\rightarrow$ One
    h. One $\rightarrow$ Many
    i. Many $\rightarrow$ One

14. Given the Weight – age curve for a human. Sketch an approximate graph:

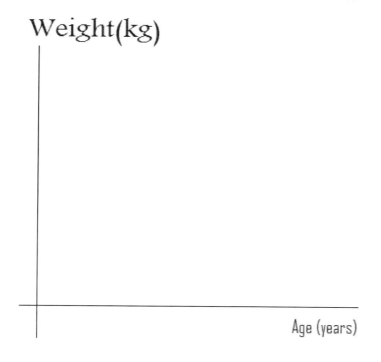

a. Weight(0) = _____ , it is the height of _____

b. Weight(t) = 10kg. t = _____

c. State its domain:_____

d. State its range: _____

15. Given the following function that describes the temperature in C° as a function of time (t = 0 corresponds to midnight):

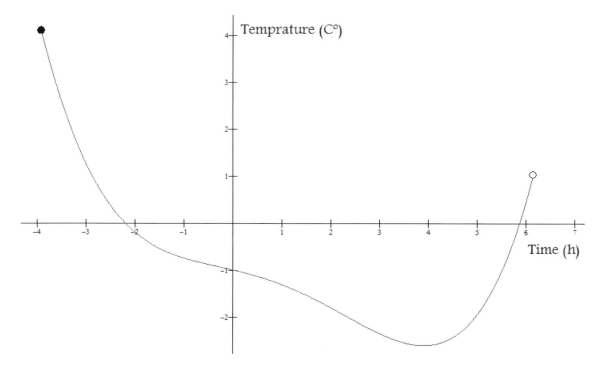

a. f(0) = _____

b. f(2) = _____ = f(__)

c. f(7) = _____

d. f(x) = 3, __ x = _____

e. f(x) = 0, __ x = _____

f. f(x) = –2 , __ x = _____

g. State its domain: _____

h. State its range: _____

i. Function increases at: _____

j. Function decreases at: _____

k. Is this function one to one? One to many? Explain.

16. Given the function the describes the change in the benefit (%) given by a certain stock:

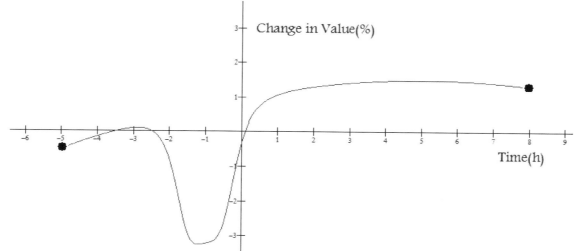

a. f(x) = 0, _x = _____

b. f(0) = _____ = f(__)

c. f(–5) = _____

d. f(1) = _____

e. f(–2) = _____ =f(__)

f. f(3) = _____

g. f(x) = –2, _x = _____

h. Is f(–2) < 0 ?

i. Is f(–2) < f(–1) ?

j. State its domain: _____

k. State its range: _____

l. Where is the function increasing? _____

m. Where is the function decreasing? _____

n. Where is the function stationary? _____

o. Is this function one to one? One to many? Explain.

17. Given the following function:

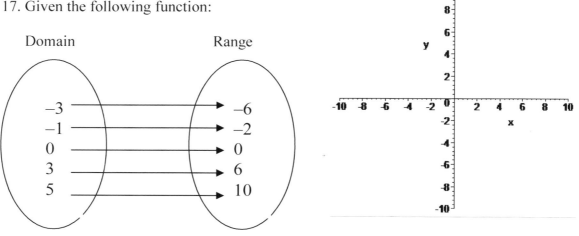

Domain   Range

-3 → -6
-1 → -2
0 → 0
3 → 6
5 → 10

a. What are the allowed values for the independent variable (The domain)?

b. What are the allowed values for the dependent variable (The range)?

c. Sketch the function on the graph.

d. Can you write a mathematical expression to express this function?

18. Given the following function:

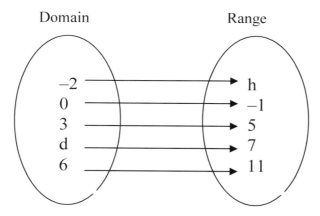

Domain   Range

-2 → h
0 → -1
3 → 5
d → 7
6 → 11

a. Can you write a mathematical expression to express this function?

b. Find h. Find d.

19. Use the graph of the gasoline consumption of a truck to answer:

a. $f(0) =$ ____

b. $f(50) =$ ____

c. $f(5) =$ ____

d. For what values of x is $f(x) = 12$

e. Is $f(60) > f(70)$?

f. For what values of x is $f(x) > 15$?

g. At what positive speed is the consumption of gasoline minimum?

h. Where is the function increasing? _____

i. Where is the function decreasing? _____

j. Where is the function stationary? _____

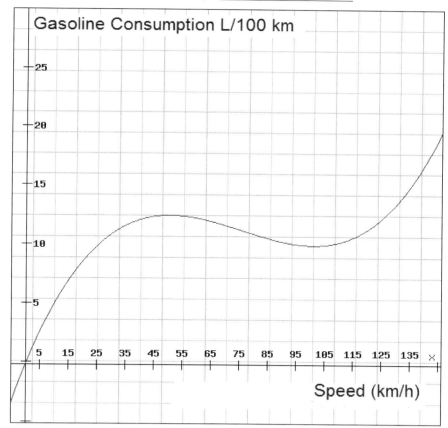

20. Functions can be represented using: _____ or _____ or _____

21. The following graph describes the concentration of a drug injected into the blood as a function of the time (in minutes) since the injection. $t = 0$ corresponds to the time of injection.

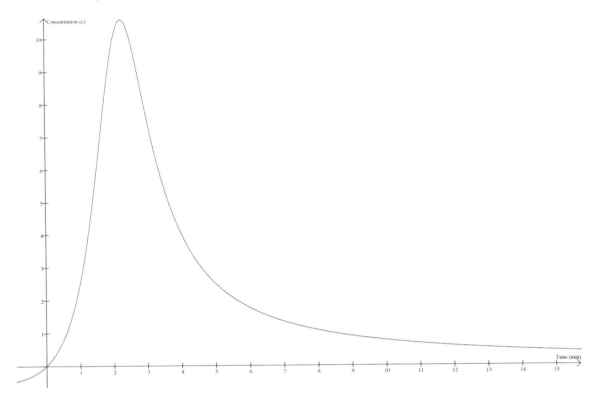

a. What is the concentration of the drug 4 hours after the injection?

b. During what period of time is the concentration increasing?

c. During what period of time is the concentration decreasing?

d. After how long is the concentration maximum?

e. When is the concentration greater than 5c?

f. When is the concentration smaller than 2c?

g. State the domain and range of the function.

22. The graph below shows the temperature in C° on a particular day as a function of time since midnight.

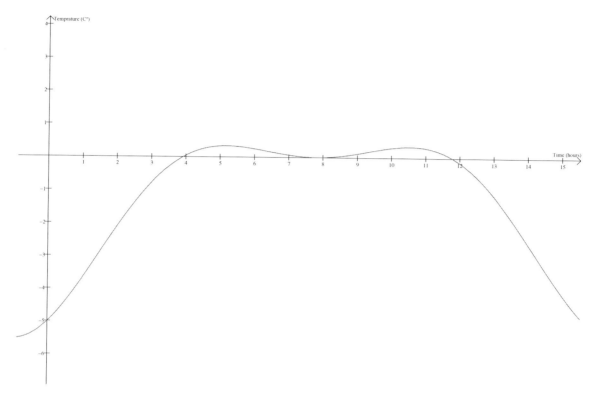

a. What was the temperature at 4:00 a.m.?

b. When was the temperature 0 degrees?

c. When was the temperature below freezing? (less than 0 degrees)

d. When was the temperature increasing?

e. When was the temperature decreasing?

f. State the domain and range of the function.

3.2. – LINEAR FUNCTIONS

1. Given the function: N(x) = 70. This function represents the number of heartbeats per second of a healthy man. Complete the following table:

x	−5	−4	−3	−2	−1	0	1	2	3	4	5
N(x)											

- Sketch the points of the chart on a graph (use a ruler).

- State the domain of the function: _____

- State the *y* intercept (sketched on the graph: (____, ____)

- State the *x* intercept: (____, ____)

- The function is increasing on the interval: _____

- The function is decreasing on the interval: _____

- Sketch the function of the graph used for the points initially drawn

- State the range of the function: _____

- The heartbeat rate is _____

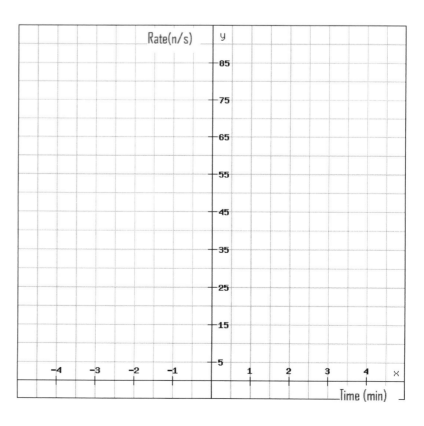

2. The position of a John in reference to his house in his afternoon walk can be modeled by the function: D(t) = 3t – 6, t is the time in hours and D is the position in km.

- Complete the following table:

t	−5	−4	−3	−2	−1	0	1	2	3	4	5
D(t)											

- Sketch the points of the chart on a graph (use a ruler).

- State the domain of the function: _____

- State the y intercept (sketched on the graph: (_____ , _____)

- State the x intercept: (_____ , _____)

- The function is increasing on the interval: _____

- The function is decreasing on the interval: _____

- Sketch the function of the graph used for the points initially drawn

- What is the speed of John _____ How is that seen on the graph?

- State the range of the function: _____

- When was John at his house? _____

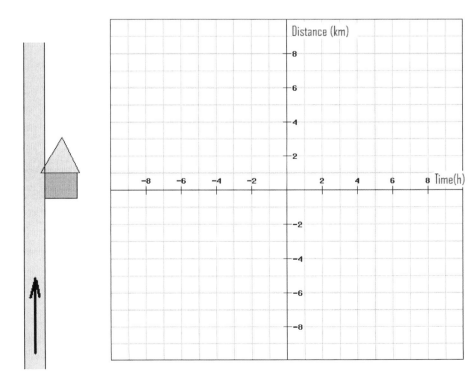

3. An elevator's behavior can be modeled by: $P(t) = -2t + 5$. Where P is the floor and t is time in minutes. The building has 15 floors and 3 parking levels below ground.

- Complete the following table:

t	−5	−4	−3	−2	−1	0	1	2	3	4	5
P(t)											

- Sketch the points of the chart on a graph (use a ruler).

- State the domain of the function: _____

- State the y intercept (sketched on the graph: (____ , ____)

- State the x intercept: (____ , ____)

- The function is increasing on the interval: _____

- The function is decreasing on the interval: _____

- Sketch the function of the graph used for the points initially drawn

- Describe the motion of the elevator _____. How is that seen on the graph?

- State the range of the function: _____

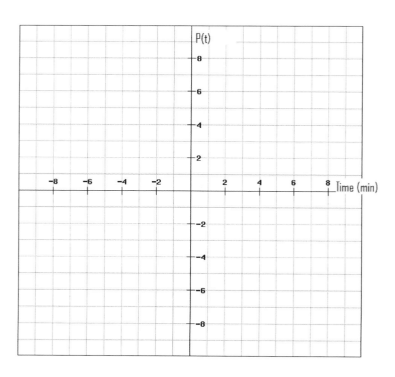

208

4. Given the function: f(x) = 4x – 3

- Complete the following table:

x	−5	−4	−3	−2	−1	0	1	2	3	4	5
f(x)											

- Sketch the points of the chart on a graph (use a ruler).

- State the domain of the function: _____

- State the y intercept (sketched on the graph: (____ , ____)

- State the x intercept: (____ , ____)

- The function is increasing on the interval: _____

- The function is decreasing on the interval: _____

- Sketch the function of the graph used for the points initially drawn

- State the range of the function: _____

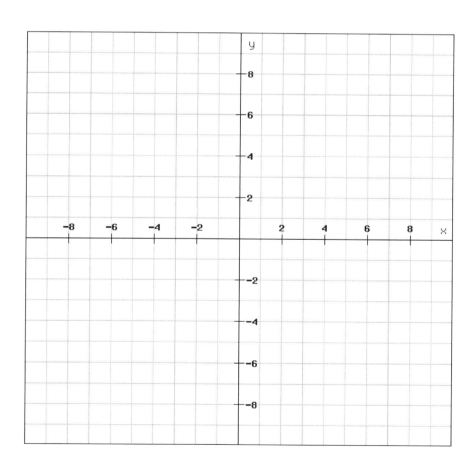

5. Given below are the equations for five different lines. Match the function with its graph.

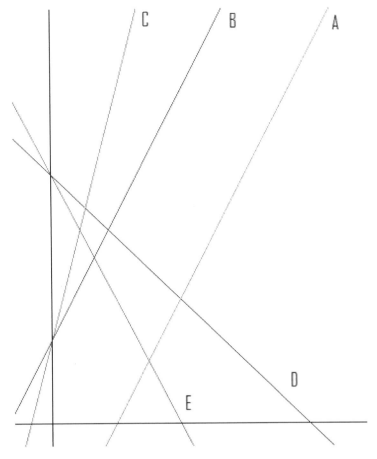

Function	On the graph
f(x) = 20 + 2x	
g(x) = 4x + 20	
s(x) = –30 + 2x	
a(x) = 60 – x	
b(x) = – 2x + 60	

6. The general functions that describes a straight line is _____

7. We know a function is a straight line because _____

8. The y–intercept (also called vertical intercept), tells us where the line crosses the

   _____. The corresponding point is of the form (,).

9. The x–intercept (also called horizontal intercept), tells us where the line crosses the

   _____. The corresponding point is of the form (,).

10. If m > 0, the line _____ left to right. If _____ the line decreases left to right.

11. In case the line is horizontal m is _____ and the line is of the form _____.

12. The larger the value of m is, the _____ the graph of the line is.

13. Given the graph, write, the slope (m), b and the equation of the line:

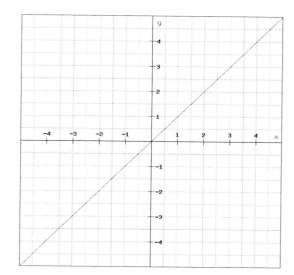

m = _____ b = _____ f(x) = _____

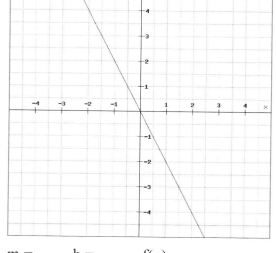

m = _____ b = _____ f(x) = _____

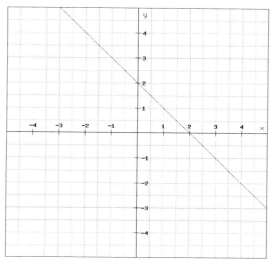

m = _____ b = _____ f(x) = _____

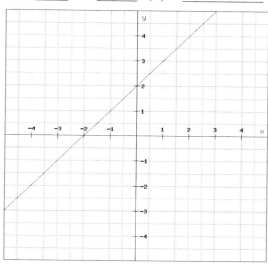

m = _____ b = _____ f(x) = _____

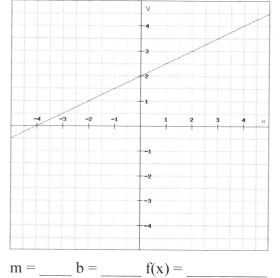

m = _____ b = _____ f(x) = _____

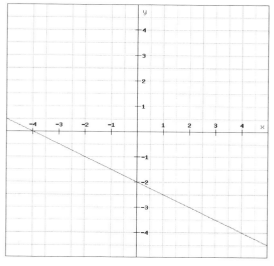

m = _____ b = _____ f(x) = _____

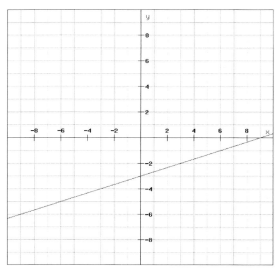

m = _____ b = _____ f(x) = _____

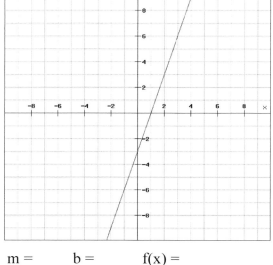

m = _____ b = _____ f(x) = _____

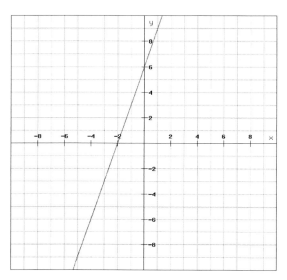

m = _____ b = _____ f(x) = _____

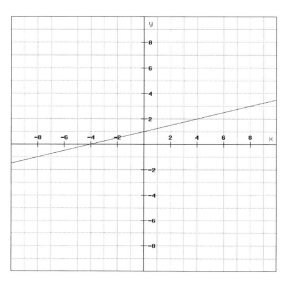

m = _____ b = _____ f(x) = _____

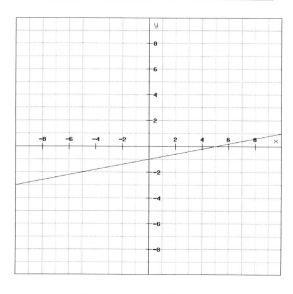

m = _____ b = _____ f(x) = _____

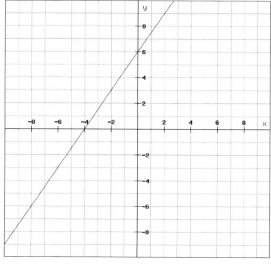

m = _____ b = _____ f(x) = _____

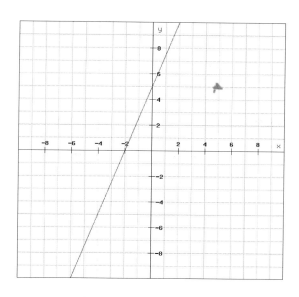

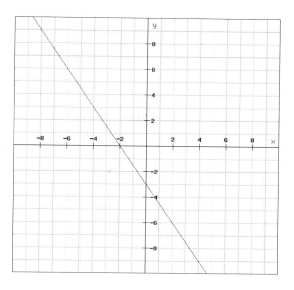

m = _____ b = _____ f(x) = _____   m = _____ b = _____ f(x) = _____

Analyze the following functions/inequlities:

1. f(x) = 1

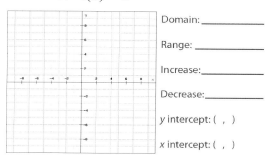

Domain: _____

Range: _____

Increase: _____

Decrease: _____

y intercept: (,)

x intercept: (,)

2. f(x) = 2

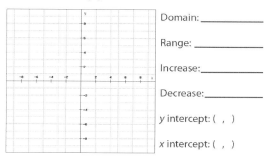

Domain: _____

Range: _____

Increase: _____

Decrease: _____

y intercept: (,)

x intercept: (,)

3. f(x) = −1

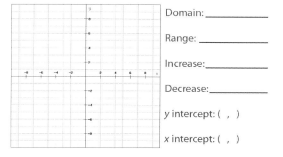

Domain: _____

Range: _____

Increase: _____

Decrease: _____

y intercept: (,)

x intercept: (,)

4. f(x) = 0

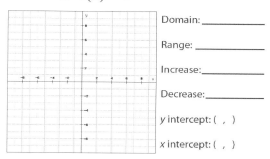

Domain: _____

Range: _____

Increase: _____

Decrease: _____

y intercept: (,)

x intercept: (,)

5. f(x) = x

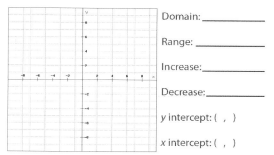

Domain: _____

Range: _____

Increase: _____

Decrease: _____

y intercept: (,)

x intercept: (,)

6. f(x) = x+1

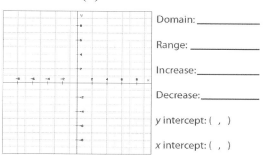

Domain: _____

Range: _____

Increase: _____

Decrease: _____

y intercept: (,)

x intercept: (,)

7. f(x) = –x

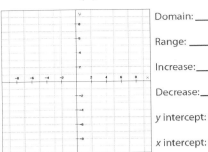

Domain:_____

Range: _____

Increase:_____

Decrease:_____

y intercept: (,)

x intercept: (,)

11. f(x) = 3 – 2x

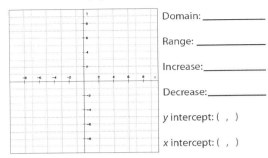

Domain:_____

Range: _____

Increase:_____

Decrease:_____

y intercept: (,)

x intercept: (,)

8. f(x) = –x–2

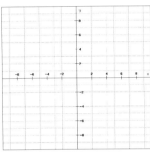

Domain:_____

Range: _____

Increase:_____

Decrease:_____

y intercept: (,)

x intercept: (,)

12. f(x) = $\dfrac{x}{3}$

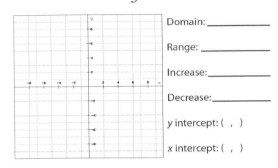

Domain:_____

Range: _____

Increase:_____

Decrease:_____

y intercept: (,)

x intercept: (,)

9. f(x) = 2x

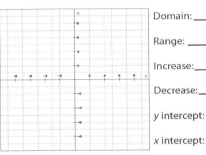

Domain:_____

Range: _____

Increase:_____

Decrease:_____

y intercept: (,)

x intercept: (,)

13. f(x) = 2x+1

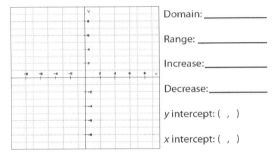

Domain:_____

Range: _____

Increase:_____

Decrease:_____

y intercept: (,)

x intercept: (,)

10. y ≤ 3x – 5

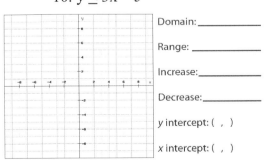

Domain:_____

Range: _____

Increase:_____

Decrease:_____

y intercept: (,)

x intercept: (,)

14. f(x) = 2x–2

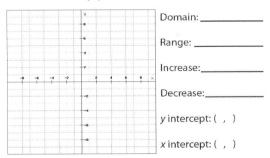

Domain:_____

Range: _____

Increase:_____

Decrease:_____

y intercept: (,)

x intercept: (,)

15. $f(x) = 3x+5$

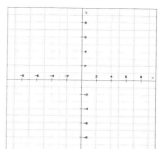

Domain:_____

Range:_____

Increase:_____

Decrease:_____

y intercept: (,)

x intercept: (,)

16. $f(x) \leq \dfrac{x}{2} - 5$

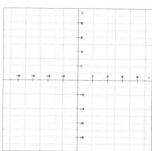

Domain:_____

Range:_____

Increase:_____

Decrease:_____

y intercept: (,)

x intercept: (,)

17. $f(x) = \dfrac{x}{4} + 6$

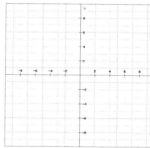

Domain:_____

Range:_____

Increase:_____

Decrease:_____

y intercept: (,)

x intercept: (,)

18. $f(x) \geq \dfrac{3x-10}{2}$

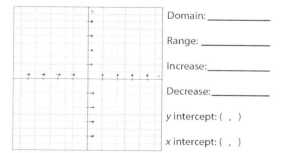

Domain:_____

Range:_____

Increase:_____

Decrease:_____

y intercept: (,)

x intercept: (,)

19. $f(x) = -\dfrac{3}{2}x - \dfrac{3}{2}$

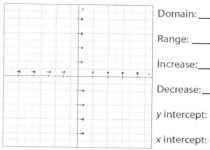

Domain:_____

Range:_____

Increase:_____

Decrease:_____

y intercept: (,)

x intercept: (,)

20. $f(x) = -\dfrac{x+3}{2}$

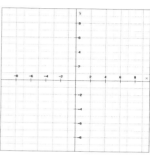

Domain:_____

Range:_____

Increase:_____

Decrease:_____

y intercept: (,)

x intercept: (,)

21. $f(x) = \dfrac{14x-1}{4}$

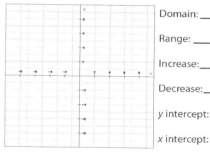

Domain:_____

Range:_____

Increase:_____

Decrease:_____

y intercept: (,)

x intercept: (,)

22. $f(x) = -\dfrac{27x-40}{15}$

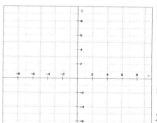

Domain:_____

Range:_____

Increase:_____

Decrease:_____

y intercept: (,)

x intercept: (,)

23. 3x + 2y = 2

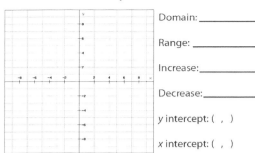

Domain: _____

Range: _____

Increase: _____

Decrease: _____

y intercept: (,)

x intercept: (,)

27. y + 2x −3 ≥ 1

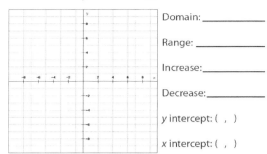

Domain: _____

Range: _____

Increase: _____

Decrease: _____

y intercept: (,)

x intercept: (,)

24. 4x− 2y −3 = 1

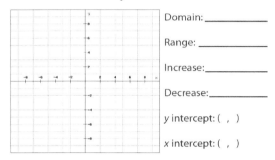

Domain: _____

Range: _____

Increase: _____

Decrease: _____

y intercept: (,)

x intercept: (,)

28. 5y + 5x = 5

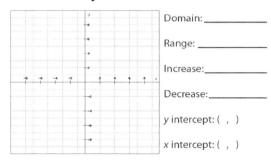

Domain: _____

Range: _____

Increase: _____

Decrease: _____

y intercept: (,)

x intercept: (,)

25. −2y + 3x = −5

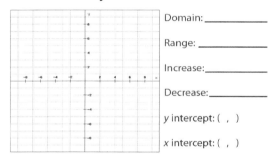

Domain: _____

Range: _____

Increase: _____

Decrease: _____

y intercept: (,)

x intercept: (,)

29. 2x − 2y −3 = 1

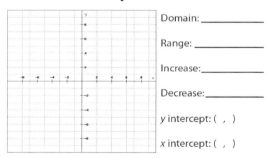

Domain: _____

Range: _____

Increase: _____

Decrease: _____

y intercept: (,)

x intercept: (,)

26. y − x ≤ 2

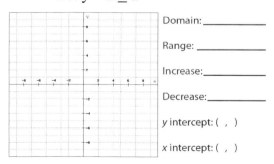

Domain: _____

Range: _____

Increase: _____

Decrease: _____

y intercept: (,)

x intercept: (,)

30. x − 2y − 150 = 0

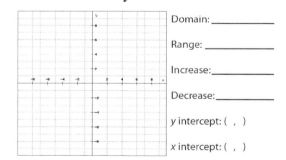

Domain: _____

Range: _____

Increase: _____

Decrease: _____

y intercept: (,)

x intercept: (,)

31. Write the equation of the line that has a slope of 2 and passes through the point (2, 4) in the forms: $y = mx + b$ and $ax + by + c = 0$, $(a, b \in Z)$

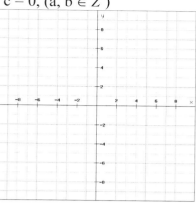

32. Write the equation of the line that has a slope of $-\dfrac{1}{2}$ and passes through the point (−2, −3) in the forms: $y = mx + b$ and $ax + by + c = 0$, $(a, b \in Z)$

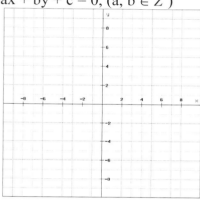

33. Write the equation of the line that has a slope of $-\dfrac{5}{2}$ and passes through the point (−1, 2) in the forms: $y = mx + b$ and $ax + by + c = 0$, $(a, b \in Z)$

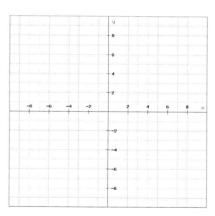

34. Find the equation of the line that passes through the points (1, 1), (2, 4), indicate its y and x intercepts and sketch it. Write its equation in the forms: y = mx + b and ax + by + c = 0, (a, b ∈ Z)

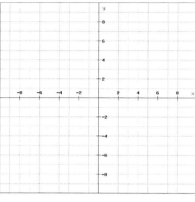

35. Find the equation of the line that passes through the points (−1, −5), (4, 3), indicate its y and x intercepts and sketch it. Write its equation in the forms: y = mx + b and ax + by + c = 0, (a, b ∈ Z)

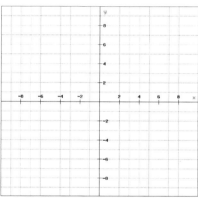

36. Find the equation of the line that passes through the points (−5, 1), (−2, 4), indicate its y and x intercepts, sketch it and write it in both formas y = mx + b and ax + by + c = 0, (a, b ∈ Z)

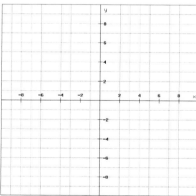

37. Write the equation of the line that is parallel to the line $y = 5x - 2$ and passes through the point $(-2, -1)$. Write its equation in the forms: $y = mx + b$ and $ax + by + c = 0$, $(a, b \in Z)$

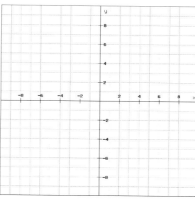

38. Write the equation of the line that is parallel to the line $y = -0.5x - 1$ and passes through the point $(-3, 6)$. Write its equation in the forms: $y = mx + b$ and $ax + by + c = 0$, $(a, b \in Z)$

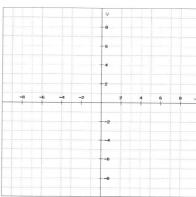

39. Sketch and write the equation of the line with a slope of $-\dfrac{1}{5}$ that passes through the point $(0,2)$.

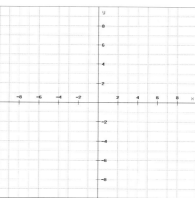

40. Sketch and write the equation of the lines with a slope: $1, 2, -3, -1, -\dfrac{1}{2}, -\dfrac{1}{3},$ that pass through the point (0,0).

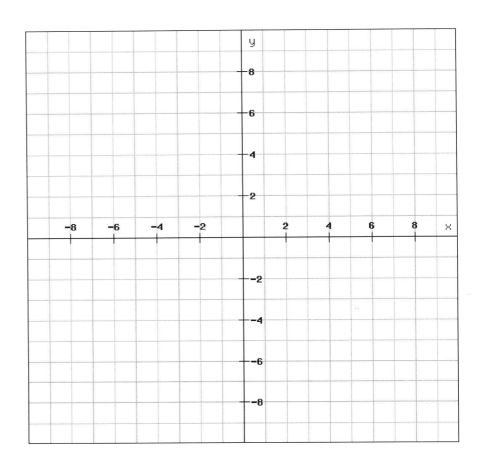

41. Sketch and write the equation of the line with a slope of –3 that passes through the point (0,–3).

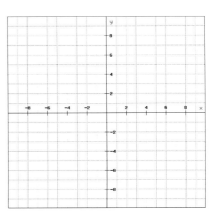

42. Sketch and write the equation of the line with a slope of 2 that passes through the point (2,0)

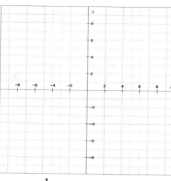

43. Sketch and write the equation of the line with a slope of $-\dfrac{1}{2}$ that passes through the point (−2,0)

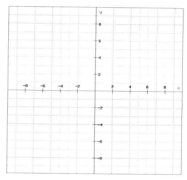

44. Sketch and write the equation of the line with a slope of 2 that passes through the point (−4,2)

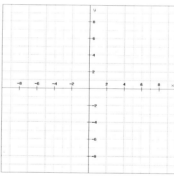

45. Find the intersection between the lines $f(x) = 2x - 3$ and $f(x) = -5x - 2$

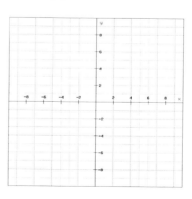

46. Find the intersection between the lines $f(x) = x - 3$ and $f(x) = x - 4$

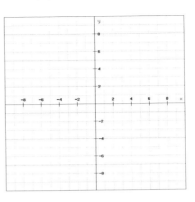

47. Find the intersection between the lines $f(x) = 2x - 3$ and $f(x) = -2x + 7$

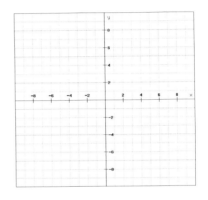

48. Find the intersection between the lines $f(x) = ax - 3$ and $f(x) = ax + 7$

49. Find the intersection between the lines $f(x) = -12x - 13$ and $f(x) = 15x + 20$.

50. Given that the lines $f(x) = 2ax - 1$ and $f(x) = 4 - 5x + 20$ do not intersect, find a.

51. Find the intersection between the lines y = 2x – 3 and 2y – 4x = – 6.

52. Given that the lines f(x) = mx – 5 and f(x) = 2x + 4 intersect at the point where x = 3, find m.

53. Given that the lines f(x) = 2x – b and f(x) = 3x + 4 intersect at the point where x = 1, find b.

54. Find the intersection between the lines 3y + 2x = 3 and 9y + 6x = 9.

55. Sketch the line $f(x) = \dfrac{-x}{2} + 3, -4 \le x < 8$

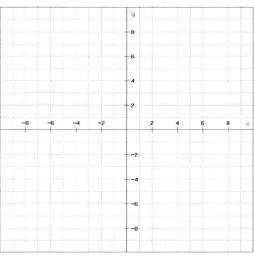

56. Given the points (1, 2) and (5, 8). Find the distance between them. Find the midpoint. Sketch to illustrate your answer.

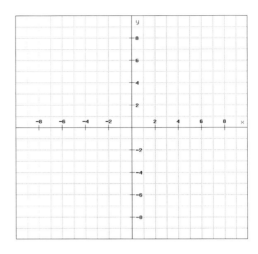

57. Given the points (–3, 2) and (5, –6). Find the distance between them. Find the midpoint. Sketch to illustrate your answer.

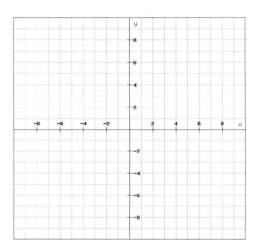

58. Given the points (–1, –6) and (–5, –1). Find the distance between them. Find the midpoint. Sketch to illustrate your answer.

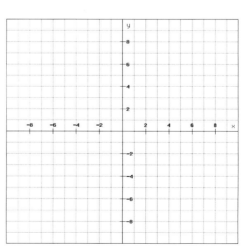

59. Given that the points $(a, -1)$ and $(5, 3)$ are 5 units away. Find a. Find the midpoint.

60. Given that the points $(1, -4)$ and $(5, c)$ are 10 units away. Find c. Find the midpoint.

61. Find the equation of all the points that are 2 units away from the origin. This

    equation describes a _____

62. Find the equation of all the points that are 5 units away from the point $(2, -1)$.

    This equation describes a _____

63. Given that the points $(1, -4)$ and $(5, c)$ are 10 units away. Find c. Find the midpoint.

64. Given the points $(-8, -7)$ and $(6, 2)$. Find the distance between them. Find the midpoint.

PERPENDICULAR LINES ($m \cdot m_\perp = -1$)

65. A slope perpendicular to 1 is _____, A slope perpendicular to 2 is _____

    A slope perpendicular to k is _____ A slope perpendicular to $\dfrac{a}{b}$ is _____

66. Find the equation of a line perpendicular to the line $y = 3x - 2$ that passes through the point (3, 12). Sketch to illustrate your answer.

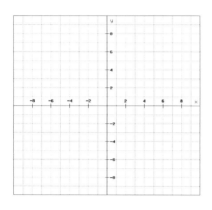

67. Find all the lines perpendicular to the line $y = -3x + 4$. Fin the ones that passes through the point (−3, 1). Sketch to illustrate your answer.

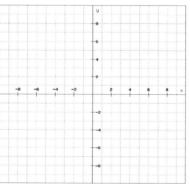

68. Find a line perpendicular to the line $y = -\dfrac{2}{5}x + 1$ that passes through the point (−1, −7). Sketch to illustrate your answer.

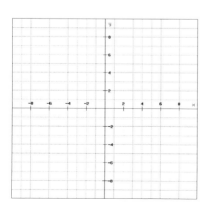

69. Given the points (–2, 5) and (4, 2).

   a. Find the equation of the line passing through them.

   b. Is the point (5, 1) on this line? Show your work.

   c. Find a perpendicular line that passes through the mid point between these points.

   d. Find all the points on the line found in c that are 0.5 units away from the point (0, 2).

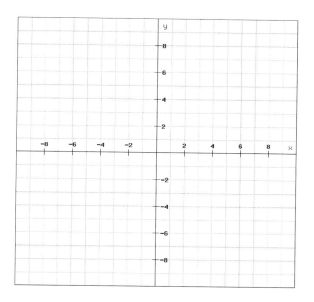

70. Find a point on the x axis that is $\sqrt{5}$ units away from the line $y = 2x + 4$

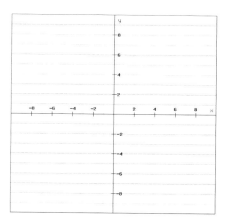

71. Find a point on the y axis that is 5 units away from the line $y = 3x + 2$

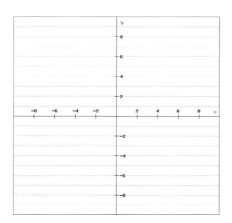

72. Given that the slope of one of the lines is 3 and that the lines are perpendicular, find the **exact** coordinates of the point of intersection of the two lines.

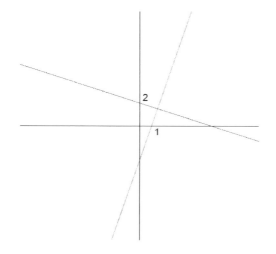

SLOPE – INTERCEPT FORM OF A LINE

73. The line $y - 3 = 2(x + 1)$ passes through the point _____ and has a slope of ____

74. The line $y + 5 = -3(x - 51)$ passes through the point _____ and has a slope of ____

75. The line $-y + 1 = (x + 3)$ passes through the point _____ and has a slope of ____

76. The line $2y + 5 = -6(x + 7)$ passes through the point _____ and has a slope of ____

77. The line $y + a = m(x + b)$ passes through the point _____ and has a slope of ____

78. The line $y - a = m(x - b)$ passes through the point _____ and has a slope of ____

79. The line $y - a = m(x + b)$ passes through the point _____ and has a slope of ____

80. Write the equation $y - 3 = 2(x + 1)$ in the explicit form

81. Write the equation $y+5=2(x+6)$ in the explicit form

82. Write down the equation of a line passing through the point (5, 2) with slope 1.

83. Write down the equation of a line passing through the point (–4, –3) with slope –2.

84. Write down the equation of a line passing through the point (6, 3) with slope $\frac{2}{3}$.

85. Write down the equation of a line passing through point (–2, –5) with slope $-\frac{2}{5}$.

86. Write down the equation of the line passing through points (–2, –5), (–7, –5),

87. Write down the equation of the line passing through points (–1, –3), (6, 5),

88. Write down the equation of the line passing through points (–1, 5), (7, –2),

APPLICATION

1. The price of a new toy (in US$) is C(t) = 20 – 0.5t, t given in days.

    a. Sketch the corresponding graph.

    b. What was the initial price of the toy? _____

    c. Find the price of the toy after 10 days

    d. What is the domain of the function, reason your answer,

    e. What is the range of the function.

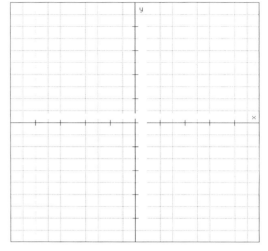

    f. What is the meaning of 0.5? Does it have units? What are they?

2. On a certain planet the temperature of the soil is 10° on the surface and 0.02° wormer with every meter of depth.

    a. Write a function to describe the temperature as a function of the depth d. State its domain and range. What are the units of the slope?

    b. Find the temperature at depth of 500m

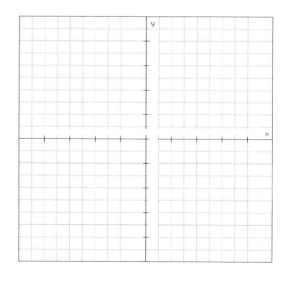

    c. Find the depth at which the temperature is 13°.

    d. Graph the function, use appropriate scale, variables and units.

3. In a factory there are 2 machines that produce a certain product. The operation cost (electricity, maintenance etc.) of Machine A is 250$ a month and the cost of production per product is 2$. The operation cost of Machine B is 200$ a month and the cost of production per product is 4$. The maximum number of products that both machines can make a month is 200.

    a. Write the functions to describe the cost C as a function of the number of products n for both machines. Indicate the domain and range of both functions. What are the units of the slope?

    b. Graph the functions, use appropriate scale, variables and units. Calculate the coordinates of important points on the graph.

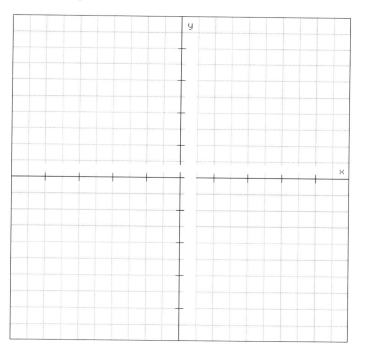

    c. Discuss in which case each machine is best.

4. A parking lot with 1200 parking spots opens at 6 am. The cars flow in a constant rate. At 10 am the parking is full.

    a. Write the function to describe the number of cars N as function of time t in hours. Indicate the domain and range of the function. What are the units of the slope?

    b. Find the number of free spots at 8:30.

    c. In case the owner needs 150 free spots at what time should he close the parking?

    d. Graph the function, use appropriate scale, variables and units.

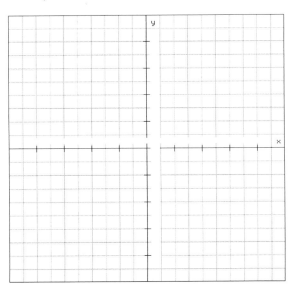

5. You need to rent a car for one day and to compare the charges of 3 different companies. Company I charges 20$ per day with additional cost of 0.20$ per mile. Company II charges 30$ per day with additional cost of 0.10$ per mile. Company III charges 60$ per day with no additional mileage charge.

    a.   Write the cost function for each one of the companies.

    b.   Sketch all 3 graphs on the same axes system.

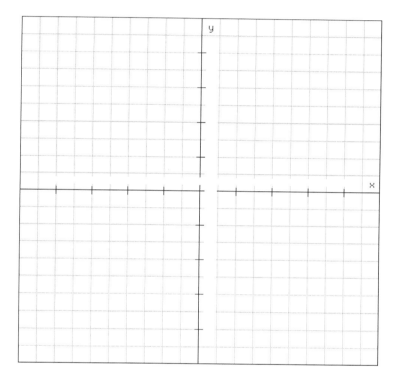

    c.   Comment on the circumstances in which renting a car from each one of the companies is best.

CHAPTER 4 - STATISTICS

4.1. – STATISTICS

In Statistics we try to obtain some conclusions by observing and/or analyzing data.

9. The set of objects that we are trying to study is called _____, the

    number of elements in the population can be _____ or _____.

10. Usually the _____ is too big and therefore we obtain a _____.

    This process is called _____.

11. We use the _____ to obtain conclusions about the _____.

Types of DATA

1. _____ data.

2. _____ data that can be divided to _____ or _____.

3. _____ can be counted while _____ data can be _____.

4. Give 3 examples of _____ data:

5. Give 3 examples of _____ _____ data:

6. Give 3 examples of _____ _____ data:

7. Given the following variables, classify them in the table:

- Eye color
- Shoe size
- Height
- Weight
- Number of cars in a parking lot
- Type of fruit

- Number of apples sold a day in a store
- Velocity of the wind
- Temperature
- Numbers of pages in a book
- Name of writer
- Number of students in a school

Categorical	Numerical Discrete	Numerical Continuous

8. In a certain class the eye color of students was studies. The following results were obtained:

Brown, Black, Brown, Blue, Brown, Black, Brown, Blue, Brown, Blue, Brown, Black, Brown, Blue.

a. How many students participated?
b. What kind of data is this?
c. Represent the information in a Bar Chart
d. Represent the information in a Pie Chart (include the %)

9. In a certain math class the following grades were obtained:

    65, 72, 85, 89, 52, 71, 89, 68, 63, 76, 61, 86, 98, 79, 79, 91, 74, 89, 77, 68, 78

    a. How many students participated?
    e. What kind of data is this?
    b. Suggest a method to represent this information in a table.
    c. Use the table to create a bar graph

10. In a certain zoo the length of a certain type of animal (in meters) was studied. The following results were obtained:

    1.77, 1.60, 1.89, 1.54, 1.77, 1.65, 1.86, 1.51, 1.67, 1.94, 1.73, 1.70, 1.66, 1.58

    a. How many animals participated?
    f. What kind of data is this?
    b. Suggest a method to represent this information in a table.
    c. Use the table to create a bar graph

11. In a certain group shoe size was studied and the following results obtained:

45, 36, 44, 38, 41, 42, 48, 39, 40, 42, 43, 41, 38, 45, 41, 38, 42, 44, 41, 41, 46

   a. How many students participated?
   b. What kind of data is this?
   c. Suggest a method to represent this information in a table.
   d. Use the table to create a bar graph

12. Choose a variable to collect information about in your classroom, state its kind, represent the information in a table and create a bar graph.

4.2. – MEAN, MEDIAN, MODE AND FREQUENCY DIAGRAMS

1. In a certain club the number of visitors per days was studied during 1 week and the following results obtained: 58, 79, 66, 78, 23, 66, 63

    a. State the number of elements in the set: _____

    b. What kind of data is this? _____

    c. Find its mean: _____   Find its mode: _____

    d. Write the data in an increasing order:

    e. Find its Median: _____   Q1 = _____ Q3 = _____

    f. Try to obtain the answers using technology.

2. In a certain restaurant the amount of meat (kg) consumed per day was studied and the following results obtained: 11.5, 12.2, 14.6, 15.0, 23.2, 21.2, 10.1, 13.1

    a. State the number of elements in the set: _____

    b. What kind of data is this? _____

    c. Find its mean: _____   Find its mode: _____

    d. Write the data in an increasing order:

    e. Find its Median: _____   Q1 = _____ Q3 = _____

    f. Try to obtain the answers using technology.

3. In a certain math class the number of exercises per day given for HW is the following: 5, 6, 6, 6, 4, 4, 5, 5, 4, 5, 6, 6, 7, 3, 0, 3

    a. State the number of elements in the set: _____

    b. What kind of data is this? _____

    c. Find its mean: _____   Find its mode: _____

    d. Write the data in an increasing order:

    e. Find its Median: _____   Q1 = _____ Q3 = _____

    f. Try to obtain the answers using technology.

4. In the following data: 2, 2, 3, 3, 9, 9, 9 one natural number is missing. It is known that the median with the missing number is 3. Find all the possible values of the missing number.

5. In a certain math class the following grades were obtained:

68, 79, 75, 89, 54, 81, 88, 62, 67, 75, 64, 85, 97, 77, 79, 90, 75, 89, 76, 68

    a. State the number of elements in the set: _____

    b. What kind of data is this? _____

    c. Find its mean: _____   Find its mode: _____

    d. Write the data in an increasing order:

    e. Find its Median: _____ $Q1 = $ _____ $Q3 = $ _____

    f. Fill the table:

Grade	Mid – Grade (Mi)	Frequency (fi)	fi x Mi	Cumulative Frequency (Fi)	Fi (%)
[51, 60]					
[61, 70]					
[71, 80]					
[81, 90]					
[91, 100]					
Total					

    g. Use the table to find the mean: _____. Comment on the result compared to the previous mean obtained.

    h. Discuss the advantages and disadvantages of organizing information in a table.

    i. Is this the only possible choice for the left column of the table? Why? Discuss the advantages and disadvantages of organizing information in such a way.

j. Design a new table with a different _____

Grade	Mid – Grade (Mi)	Frequency (fi)	Fi x Mi	Cumulative Frequency (Fi)	Fi (%)

k. Use the table to find the mean: _____. Comment on the result compared to the previous mean obtained.

l. The mean of the <u>population</u> is denoted with the Greek letter mu: _____

and typically it is _____. The mean of the <u>sample</u> is denoted by

_____

m. Find the modal interval in both tables:

1st: _____ 2nd: _____

n. In general this method of organizing information is called _____

o. The 1st column is called _____ with upper interval boundary and

_____ interval boundary.

p. The 2nd column is called _____

q. On the following grid paper sketch the corresponding points.

Fi: Cumulative frequency

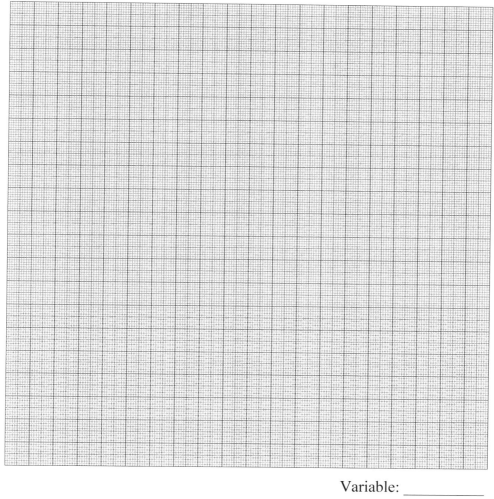

Variable: _____

r. This graph is called cumulative frequency curve or _____

s. Find the median using the graph: _____

t. Find the first quartile (Q_1) using the graph: Q_1 = _____

u. Find the third quartile (Q_3) using the graph: Q_3 = _____

v. Find P_{30} using the graph: _____ Find P_{70} using the graph: _____

w. The <u>Inter Quartile Range</u> is in general _____ in this case it is _____

x. Try to obtain the answers using technology.

6. In a certain class the following heights (in m) of students were collected:

1.77, 1.60, 1.89, 1.54, 1.77, 1.65, 1.86, 1.51, 1.67, 1.94, 1.73, 1.70, 1.66, 1.70

a. State the number of elements in the set: _____

b. What kind of data is this? _____

c. Find its mean: _____   Find its mode: _____

d. Write the data in an increasing order:

e. Find its Median: _____   Q1 = _____ Q3 = _____

f. Fill the table:

Grade	Mid – Grade (Mi)	Frequency (fi)	fi x Mi	Cumulative Frequency (Fi)	Fi (%)
[1.50 – 1.60)					
[1.60 – 1.70)					
[1.70– 1.80)					
[1.80 – 1.90)					
[1.90 – 2.00)					
Total					

g. Use the table to find the mean: _____. Comment on the result compared to the previous mean obtained.

h. Discuss the advantages and disadvantages of organizing information in a table.

i. Is this the only possible choice for the left column of the table? Why? Discuss the advantages and disadvantages of organizing information in such a way.

j. On the following grid paper sketch the corresponding points.

Fi: Cumulative frequency

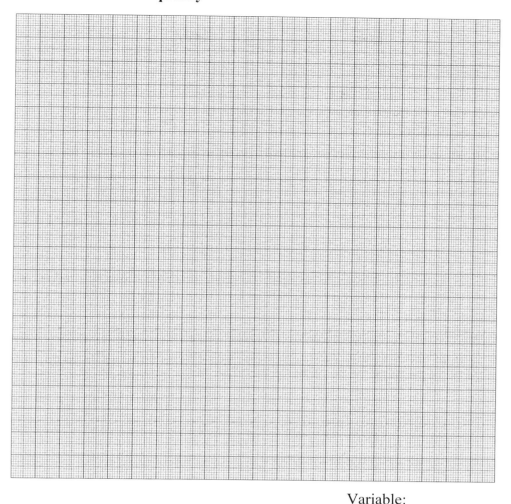

Variable: _____

k. This graph is called cumulative frequency curve or _____

l. Find the median using the graph: _____

m. Find the first quartile (Q_1) using the graph: Q_1 = _____

n. Find the third quartile (Q_3) using the graph: Q_3 = _____

o. Find P_{30} using the graph: _____ Find P_{70} using the graph: _____

p. The <u>Inter Quartile Range</u> is in general _____ in this case it is _____

q. Try to obtain the answers using technology.

7. In a certain class students eye color was collected:

   Brown, Black, Brown, Blue, Brown, Blue, Green, Brown, Black, Green

   a. State the number of elements in the set: _____

   b. What kind of data is this? _____

   c. Fill the table:

Eye Color	Mid – Color (Mi)	Frequency (fi)	fi x Mi	Cumulative Frequency (Fi)	Fi (%)
Brown					
Blue					
Green					
Black					
Total					

   d. Obtain the mean: _____

   e. State the mode of the set: _____

   f. Find the modal interval: _____

   g. Find the Median using the original data: _____

   h. Find the median using the table, discuss your answer.

   i. Find the answers to all the different parts using your GDC.

   j. Represent the data in a histogram:

4.3. – PROBABILITY

Probability is the science of chance or likelihood of an event happening

If a random experiment is repeated _____ times in such a way that each of the trials is identical and independent, where n(A) is the number of _____ event A occurred,

then: Relative frequency of event A $= P(A) = \dfrac{n(A)}{N}$ $(N \to \infty)$

Exercises

1. In an unbiased coin what is P(head) ?

    This probability is called _____.

2. Explain the difference between theoretical probability and experimental probability.

3. Throw a drawing pin and fill the table:

	Fell pointing upwards	Fell on its side	Total number of throws
Number of events			
Probability			

4. The definition of probability ("*Laplace law*")is:

    $P(A) = \dfrac{Number \rule{6cm}{0.4pt}}{Total \rule{6cm}{0.4pt}}$

Properties of probability

   $0 \leq P(A) \leq$ ____

   $P(U) =$ ____

5. Given the sentence "Good day everyone". Find the following probabilities in case the choices are being made in a random way:

   a. P(choosing a vowel) =

   c. P(choosing a "e") =

   b. P(choosing a "o") =

   d. P(choosing a "z") =

6. In case a student is chosen randomly in your classroom. Find the probability it´s a girl.

7. Find the probability of getting a prime number sum on tossing 2 dice.

8. Find the probability of getting a sum of 17 on tossing 3 dice.

9. Find the probability of being left handed in your classroom.

10. Find the probability of obtaining a sum of 5 on tossing 2 dice.

11. Find the probability of obtaining 2 tails on tossing 2 coins.

12. Find the probability that a 2 digit number divides by 3

13. Find the probability of choosing the letter b in the word probability

14. Find the probability of choosing a number that contains the digit 7 in the first hundred numbers (1 to 100).

15. Find the probability of choosing a number that contains only even digits in the first thousand numbers (1 to 1000).

16. Knowing that the sum of 2 dice is more than 5, find the probability it's 10

CHAPTER 5

5.1. – INTERNATIONAL SYSTEM OF UNITS

1. Meter(m) is a unit of _____ Other units of _____ are: _____

2. Meter square (m^2) is a unit of _____ Other units of _____ are: _____

3. An area has units of _____ A length has units of _____

4. Kilo = ___ Mili = ___

Convert the units, use scientific notation in at least one of each type of exercises:

5. How many metres in 2.5 km?

6. How many metres in 0.5 km?

7. How many metres^2 in $\frac{1}{3}$ km^2?

8. How many metres in 56 km?

9. How many metres in 2500 km?

10. How many km^2 in 26 m^2?

11. How many km in 75 m?

12. How many km in 1000 m?

13. How many m in $5.2 \cdot 10^7$ km?

14. How many km^2 in $5.12 \cdot 10^8$ m^2?

15. How many mm in 3.04 m?

16. How many mm^2 in 0.5 m^2?

17. How many mm^2 in 1 m^2?

18. How many mm in 2 m?

19. How many mm in 2.5 m?

20. How many mm^2 are 1.35 m^2?

21. How many cm in $\frac{1}{3}$ m?

22. How many cm^2 in 56 m^2?

23. How many cm in 3.1 km?

24. How many mm^2 in 0.5 cm^2?

25. How many cm in in 120 m?

26. How many mm^2 in 5.1 cm^2?

27. How many cm in 17 km?

28. How many m in 12392 km?

29. How many mm^2 in 5.1 m^2?

30. How many m^2 in 2.2 mm^2?

31. How many cm in 13.12 m?

32. Complete the table:

mm	cm	m	km
14			
	65		
		3	
			5
12.5			
	3.7		
		4.78	
			1.31
			0.008
mm^2	cm^2	m^2	Km^2
14			
	65		
		3	
			5
12.5			
	3.7		
		4.78	
			1.31
			0.008

5.2. – COMMON ERRORS

1. $\sqrt{A+B} = \sqrt{A} + \sqrt{B}$ True / False, Give an example to show your answer.

2. $\sqrt{A^2 + B^2} = A + B$ True / False, Give an example to show your answer.

3. $(A+B)^2 = A^2 + B^2$ True / False, if false write the correct version.

4. $(A+B)(A-B) = A^2 + B^2$ True / False, Give an example to show your answer.

5. $(A+B)(A-B) = A^2 - B^2$ True / False, if false write the correct version..

6. $(x+2)^2 = x^2 + 4x + 2$ True / False, if false write the correct version.

7. $(A-B)^2 = A^2 - B^2$ True / False, Give an example to show your answer.

8. $(2x-3)^2 = 4x^2 - 6x + 9$ True / False, if false write the correct version.

9. $(\sqrt{a} - 3)^2 = a^2 - 6a + 9$ True / False, if false write the correct version.

10. $x^2 x^3 = x^6$ True / False, if false write the correct version.

11. $(x^2)^3 = x^{(2^3)}$ True / False, if false write the correct version.

12. $\dfrac{x^{10}}{x^2} = x^5$ True / False, if false write the correct version.

13. $x^1 = 1$ True / False, if false write the correct version.

14. $x^0 = 0$ True / False, if false write the correct version.

15. $-3^2 = (-3)^2$ True / False, if false write the correct version.

16. $(4x^2) = (4x)^2$ True / False, if false write the correct version.

17. $\sqrt{7x} = 7x^{\frac{1}{2}}$ True / False, if false write the correct version.

18. $\dfrac{0}{2} = \dfrac{2}{0}$ True / False, if false write the correct version.

19. $\dfrac{14+x}{14} = x$ True / False, if false write the correct version.

20. $\dfrac{7-x}{7} = x-1$ True / False, if false write the correct version.

21. $\dfrac{a+b}{a} = 1 + \dfrac{b}{a}$ True / False, if false write the correct version.

22. $\dfrac{14+x}{14} = x + \dfrac{x}{14}$ True / False, if false write the correct version.

23. $\dfrac{1}{x+y} = \dfrac{1}{x} + \dfrac{1}{y}$ True / False, if false write the correct version.

24.   An **expression** and an **equation** is the same thing.   True / False

25. $\dfrac{\left(\dfrac{a}{b}\right)}{c} = \dfrac{a}{\left(\dfrac{b}{c}\right)}$ True / False, if false write the correct version.

26. $-a^2 = (-a)^2$ True / False, if false write the correct version.

27. $a^{-2} = (-a)^2$ True / False, if false write the correct version.

28. $a^{-2} = -a^2$ True / False, if false write the correct version.

29. $a^{-2} = -\dfrac{1}{a^2}$ True / False, if false write the correct version.

30. $a^{-2} = \dfrac{1}{a^2}$ True / False, if false write the correct version.

31. $a^{-1} = -\dfrac{1}{a}$ True / False, if false write the correct version.

32. $\dfrac{1}{2} + \dfrac{1}{3} = \dfrac{1}{2+3}$ True / False, if false write the correct version.

33. $a^{-1} + a^{-1} = a^{-2}$ True / False, if false write the correct version.

34. $a^{-1}a^{-1} = a^{-2}$ True / False, if false write the correct version.

35. $a^{-2}a^{-3} = a^{-6}$ True / False, if false write the correct version.

36. $a^{-2} + a^{-3} = a^{-5}$ True / False, if false write the correct version.

Made in the USA
Middletown, DE
13 September 2015